When your panty product is dying what do you do? You change the agency, of course?

How about 2 less commercials per month and more R+D for your product.

✓ *"We are the greatest innovators on earth. So what happened?"*

Up Against The (Judy) Wald

By Julie Baumgold

When Judy Wald was a little girl she rode through the Bowery Friday evenings before sundown in her immigrant grandfather's open Bentley throwing gold coins to the snarl of poor folk. It was the perfect training for a Jewish Princess and probably the last time in her life Judy gave away something for nothing. She felt the chummy little glow that power can bring as her tiny fist dipped into the big pouch of coins on the seat.

Forty years later, after four husbands, death and travail and cutting frozen fish dinners in half to make them last another day, Judy Wald again feels the power thrill. As well she might. Judy Wald is the *eminence grise* of advertising. Neverneverland's _____ the business called _____ gathered a stable _____ which she has _____ agencies. She is _____ castle, with a _____ all a-grovel. _____ aw from a _____ st 40's—person- _____ n Avenue; but in _____ d has had her own _____ branches in Lon- _____ Angeles. She made _____ t personnel place- _____ Walter Thompson, _____ ed her to revamp _____ creative people. _____ plan," Judy purrs _____ corrugated paper _____ a snit, the voice _____ Fred Capossella

_____ of Judy Wald as _____ cy for advertising _____ n only one _____ . Under a

Jeff Metzner,
vice president and
associate creative director,
Daniel and Charles

Gene Case,
senior partner,
Jack Tinker and
Partners

Bob Wilvers,
senior partner,
Jack Tinker and
Partners

RADIO PUBLIC RELATIONS

THE REAL
MADMEN

Copyright © 2011, Elwin Street Productions

Conceived and produced by
Elwin Street Productions
144 Liverpool Road
London N1 1LA
www.elwinstreet.com

First published in the United States in 2011 by Running Press Book
Publishers, A Member of the Perseus Books Group.

Printed in China

Books published by Running Press are available at special discounts for bulk
purchases in the United States by corporations, institutions, and other
organizations. For more information, please contact the Special Markets
Department at the Perseus Books Group, 2300 Chestnut Street, Suite 200,
Philadelphia, PA 19103, or call (800) 810-4145, ext. 5000, or e-mail
special.markets@perseusbooks.com.

ISBN 978-0-7624-4090-0
Library of Congress Control Number: 2011926064

9 8 7 6 5 4 3 2 1
Digit on the right indicates the number of this printing

Running Press Book Publishers
2300 Chestnut Street
Philadelphia, PA 19103-4371
Visit us on the web!
www.runningpress.com

PICTURE CREDITS

Reproduction of images
authorized by:

Advertising Archives: pp. 98
(bottom right), 99 (bottom)
Alamy: front flap, 123
Amil Gargano: pp. 133, 137, 139
Avis Rent-a-car: p. 128
Bayer HealthCare LLC: p. 189
Bimbo Bakeries USA, Inc: p. 67
Chivas Brothers: p. 127
Corbis Images: pp. 171, 201
Coyne & Blanchard, Inc., DBA
Communication Arts: pp. 174–175
DDB Worldwide Communication
Group Inc.: pp. 59, 67, 81
Duke University, North Carolina:
p. 27
El Al Israel Airlines: p. 81
George Lois: pp. 105, 111, 112,
113, 115, 119, 168, 169
Getty Images: pp. 4, 15, 31, 49,
53, 69, 75, 83, 101, 145, 193
iStockphoto: p. 11

Jon Williamson: p. 19
Judith Wald: p. 157
Kathryn Krone: p. 89
Lyndon Baines Johnson Library,
Texas: p. 163
McCann Erickson: p. 183
McDermott Library, The
University of Texas: pp. 205, 206
Ogilvy & Mather: pp. 35 (left),
38, 39 (top right and bottom left),
42, 43, 45
PLR IP Holdings, LLC: pp. 78, 79
Talon International: pp. 152, 153
The Hertz Corporation: pp. 142,
143
The Procter & Gamble Company:
p. 197
Viyella: p. 39 (top left)
Volkswagen Zubehör: pp. 94, 95,
98 (top and bottom left), 99 (top)
Volvo Car Corporation: p. 136.
Wisconsin Historical Society: p.
35 (right)
Young & Rubicam: p. 179

Figures featured on the
endpapers include: Front—Bill
Bernbach, Gene Case, DDB,
Amil Gargano, Helmut Krone,
Jeff Metzner, PKL, Jack Tinker,
Judith Wald, Bob Wilvers, Young
& Rubicam, and Bernie Zlotnick.
Back—21 Club, Carl Ally, Jerry
Della Femina, Carl Fischer,
Gilbert Advertising, George Lois
Ron Rosenfeld, and Young &
Rubicam.

With thanks to the following for
supplying endpaper images: Carl
Fischer, Amil Gargano, Kathryn
Krone, Bob Kuperman, George
Lois, McCann Erickson, Judith
Wald, and Bernie Zlotnick, 21
Club, DDB Worldwide
Communication Group Inc., El
Al Israel Airlines, Carl Fischer,
Richard Gilbert, George Lois,
Judith Wald, Bernie Zlotnick.

THE REAL
MADMEN

THE RENEGADES OF MADISON AVENUE AND
THE GOLDEN AGE OF ADVERTISING

ANDREW CRACKNELL
FOREWORD BY SIR JOHN HEGARTY

RUNNING PRESS
PHILADELPHIA • LONDON

Contents

DEDICATION

To the gentle Dan Levin, my group head at CDP, because he
gave me my first break, taught me with immense skill and
patience, and set me on the road; because he introduced me
to the US advertising of this era and explained its importance;
and a little because in 1967 he had an E Type Jaguar and that
was all the incentive I needed. Sadly he died in October 2010.

AUTHOR'S NOTE

In his 1964 novel *The Advertising Man*, Jack Dillon makes one passing reference to
those then employed in advertising on New York's Madison Avenue as "Mad Men."
Apart from that, I found no evidence that the expression was in any sort of use until
the AMC series of that name. For that reason, and to avoid confusion, throughout this
book the phrase will refer only to people, events, attitudes, and images in the TV
drama and not the world of 1960s New York advertising.

All quoted material is either referenced directly in the text, or can be found in the
sources provided at the back of the book.

Foreword BY SIR JOHN HEGARTY

Advertising is a wonderful business in that it recognizes talent very quickly. It applauds it, rewards it, and promotes it. The only problem is, it also forgets it very quickly.

The word "history" in our industry is almost a dirty word. We're obsessed with tomorrow and the next big thing. In many ways that's what makes it so exciting. Constant invention is at its core. Creativity is, after all, about breaking something down and putting something new in its place.

But sometimes this can work against it. I was lucky enough to be taught history by an inspirational teacher who's mantra was "history isn't about the past, it's about the future." Understanding where we came from, why we did what we did, and how it could influence tomorrow was at the heart of his teaching.

It is this that makes this book so special.

Yes, it is about the past. It's about a moment in time when everything changed and modern advertising was born. It will make you laugh and wonder at the characters that inhabit these pages, and teach you how to recognize true creativity as opposed to the illusion of it.

It will also give you an insight in how to run a creative company, and make sure it continues to be successful—Bernbach's brilliantly insightful letter to his staff about the dangers of bigness and conformity should be plastered across the walls of any creative organization. Not that this is a "how to" book. Far from it. But like any great story it carries within it lessons that go beyond the intended narrative.

Andrew Cracknell's writing captures the passion, madness, and mayhem that is all part of a creative revolution; the courage and determination it takes to succeed and, most of all, how to conjure magic out of nothing.

How true is Mad Men?

BY FRED DANZIG

You don't have to be an adman to love the Creative Revolution. All that's required is an appreciation of how Madison Avenue's ad agencies veered from "hard sell" advertising in the 1960s, abandoning brain-jarring repetition and hyperbole, creating instead a softer, more colloquial "selling" premise. Radiating good taste, humor, "real"-looking people, and down-to-earth copy, their amiable messages began relating more directly to real everyday life in America.

Cut to July 2007, and the debut of the AMC cable network's *Mad Men* series, billed as a serious recreation of Madison Avenue in the sixties, when the Creative Revolution was reenergizing ad agencies. Most admen who survived that decade and tuned in to *Mad Men* were hoping it would reflect the energy that was coursing through the business during that decade. But the TV version instead focuses on a fictitious "new" agency, Sterling Cooper Draper Pryce, that is curiously immune to the energizing creative work going on all around it at smaller, less stuffy "start-ups."

Mad Men did succeed, however, in opening memory floodgates; veteran Creative Revolution pioneers were asked to reminisce, and now, in these pages, Andrew Cracknell brings them together to provide the real-life details and contrasts to the *Mad Men* storyline. With the back stories of landmark ad campaigns here, we witness a shift from musty old agency dos and don'ts (i.e., "leave room in the ad for the logo") to the challenging "fresh ideas only" approach. Agency writers and artists, no longer confined to separate cubicles, would henceforth work together as teams, in one office.

As the new ads won acclaim—and increased sales—young men and women started to take notice. And when they began setting off in pursuit of "real world" careers, many were drawn to the agency business.

How to break in? What about the "social barriers"? This Revolution was breaking down those barriers. Andrew Cracknell describes the paths many future advertising legends had to follow to get their first jobs, and how they would later open doors for others. Many of them bore vowel-rich ethnic names that were notably missing from agency office nameplates. Their stories are universally applicable; learn from them.

Mad Men, to its credit, reflects this aspect of the Madison Avenue world. We see Don Draper take himself from selling fur coats to ad agency partner despite having no family connections or elite school pedigree to ease his way. And we also see his secretary, Peggy Olson, parlay her creative ideas into an office of her own.

WHEN I JOINED *Advertising Age* in New York as senior editor in 1962, the Creative Revolution's fresh work was already the talk of the business. These game-changing campaigns had begun transforming the business during the fifties, most notably after Doyle Dane Bernbach's "Think Small" newspaper ad for the Volkswagen "Bug" came along. Its copy delivered a refreshing sermon about simplicity in life—and this to a nation with a "big-bigger-biggest" obsession. Ironically, *Mad Men* had a scene that took note of this ad. Don Draper—the agency's creative leader, remember—reads the "Think Small" ad for the first time. He hates it. Some forty years later, a panel of experts will vote it "Best Advertising of the Twentieth Century."

To be fair, *Mad Men* never pretends to be a documentary film. It's committed to story lines and pure entertainment, smartly focusing on the lives and loves of its central characters and their hallowed clients. While it deservedly wins awards (thirteen Emmys among them, and counting), those awards aren't coming from Madison Avenue.

Here, then, we have this book to flesh out the story, written by an adman who has lived the life. It traces the tale back to 1949, with the upstart Doyle Dane Bernbach agency's redefining advertising content. The creative competition that ensued peaked in the sixties, when young writers and artists were saying, "Let's open our own agency; let's show 'em how it's done."

"In advertising, we know how to construct the body, but the real trick is in knowing how to run blood through the veins."

BILL BERNBACH

Have a read of the letter across the page.

Although written by a man who turned out to be an absolute master of persuasive communication, it failed to persuade. Ironically its subject matter was an analysis of how its recipients, the management of an advertising agency where persuasion should be all, were going wrong, and what they should do to put it right. It was written in 1947 by Bill Bernbach, the creative director, to his colleagues on the board of Grey Advertising, a midsized New York agency. It was, as far as we can gather, totally ignored.

It's a moot point as to whether Bernbach would have ever been able to wring all he wanted out of an uninspired and uninspiring Grey so we'll never know what would have happened if they'd bought into his ideas. But certainly no steps were taken to accommodate his beliefs or adhere to his suggested policies. Spurned, Bernbach took matters into his own hands, put into practice what his letter preached and wrought as fundamental a revolution on processes and product as ever occurred in any business activity; and this all spread from one initially tiny organization in one small corner of a very large and still growing business.

It's worth reading in full. Its dazzling lucidity and heartfelt concerns are not usually the stuff of an interdepartmental memo. And reasonable and

May 15, 1947

Dear _____:

Our agency is getting big. That's something to be happy about. But it's
something to worry about, too, and I don't mind telling you I'm damned
worried. I'm worried that we're going to fall into the trap of bigness,
that we're going to worship techniques instead of substance, that we're
going to follow history instead of making it, that we're going to be
drowned by superficialities instead of buoyed up by solid fundamentals.
I'm worried lest hardening of the creative arteries begin to set in.

There are a lot of great technicians in advertising. And unfortunately
they talk the best game. They know all the rules. They can tell you that
people in an ad will get you greater readership. They can tell you that
a sentence should be this sort or that long. They can tell you that body
copy should be broken up for easier reading. They can give you fact
after fact after fact. They are the scientists of advertising. But
there's one little rub. Advertising is fundamentally persuasion and
persuasion happens to be not a science, but an art.

It's that creative spark that I'm so jealous of for our agency and
that I am so desperately fearful of losing. I don't want academicians.
I don't want scientists. I don't want people who do the right things.
I want people who do inspiring things.

In the past year I must have interviewed about eighty people--writers
and artists. Many of them were from the so-called giants of the agency
field. It was appalling to see how few of these people were genuinely
creative. Sure, they had advertising know-how. Yes, they were up on
advertising technique.

But look beneath the technique and what did you find? A sameness,
a mental weariness, a mediocrity of ideas. But they could defend every
ad on the basis that it obeyed the rules of advertising. It was like
worshiping a ritual instead of the God.

All this is not to say that technique is unimportant. Superior
technical skill will make a good man better. But the danger is a
preoccupation with technical skill or the mistaking of technical skill
for creative ability.

The danger lies in the temptation to buy routinized men who have a
formula for advertising. The danger lies in the natural tendency to
go after tried-and-true talent that will not make us stand out in
competition but rather make us look like all the others.

If we are to advance we must emerge as a distinctive personality. We
must develop our own philosophy and not have the advertising philosophy
of others imposed on us.

Let us blaze new trails. Let us prove to the world that good taste,
good art, and good writing can be good selling.

Respectfully,
Bill Bernbach

emollient though its phrases seem, it's a catalogue of dynamite heresies, the relentless destruction of all the practices and beliefs held as inalienable wisdom by its addressees at the time. He was a curious man in a curious business. On the receiving end of advertising, as we all are minute by minute, it's difficult to see how anyone can get really worked up about it. It's just there, like weather and noise and things made of plastic.

It's only ads. In their creation, no one dies, no one even gets hurt, apart from the occasional bruised ego and crushed vanity. At best it's fluffy entertainment, at worst an insulting, mindless assault, a disposable means to a bigger end. Ideologically, depending on your own political stance, it's the rattling of a stick in a bucket of swill—George Orwell—or a useful tool, but merely a tool, of capitalism. An adjunct. It does not, would not, exist in its own right.

Even within advertising its practitioners often have a morosely realistic view of their role in society. Julian Koenig, one of the key figures in this story, recently expressed his regret that he'd spent his life in its pursuit, happy that he'd done it extremely well but less so that he'd done it at all; a French advertising executive published his autobiography utilizing an old and well-worn advertising gag: "Don't tell my mother I work in advertising, she thinks I'm the piano player in a brothel."

It's not a business inside which you'd expect a passionate battle of competing philosophies and ideas to create volcanic heat and upheaval, still resonating sixty years later. And yet you can see the emotion it aroused in Bill Bernbach, especially when he thought it wasn't going the way he so strongly thought it should. Strongly enough that in 1949, aged thirty-eight, an age when senior managers should be cozily slipping their feet further and further under their executive desks, Bernbach left his secure and successful job as creative director to follow his utter conviction that there was a better way to do things—and started his own agency.

Perhaps surprisingly in such a competitive business, his beliefs were not just about performance, efficacy, and success, but about the role of advertising as an intrusive force for better or for worse in the life of contemporary society. Although in interviews he would often claim that to make ads more entertaining was simply a better way to get the consumer on your side and thus more likely to be persuaded, his concerns were as much rooted in ethics as they were in efficiency. You can gauge the humanity in the man by this, one of his many quotes respected not just for their content but also their precision of thought and expression:

"All of us who professionally use the mass media are the shapers of society. We can vulgarize that society. We can brutalize it. Or we can help lift it onto a higher level."

And note also the last sentence of the letter. He didn't have to include "good taste" in his recipe; all advertisers have always been concerned with "what" they say but few ever worry too much about "how" they say it, as long as it achieves maximum results. But he was clearly dismayed by the crassness and soullessness of the advertising prevalent at that time simply because it *was* crass and soulless, and he saw that as socially corrosive, or at least debilitating.

He believed there was a better way for America's corporations to treat their customers. Like a good theater playwright or director, he appreciated the audience was not an inert, inactive recipient but a living organism whose very reception of the message affected the message itself. He saw a lighter way, a more humorous, demotic way, that said, "Hey, we're all in this together; you know we're going to try and sell you something—let's both enjoy the process."

BERNBACH IS AN UNLIKELY HERO. Although not lacking in confidence, he could not be described as charismatic. Perhaps his most commanding asset was a pair of piercing blue eyes; certainly there was nothing else about him that demanded instant respect, short, rotund, and average-looking as he was. And yet more than sixty years later, advertising people all over the world, some entering the business two generations after he died, still talk of him with reverence. After his death in October 1982, *Harper's* magazine told its readers he "probably had a greater impact on American culture than any of the distinguished writers and artists who have appeared in the pages of *Harper's* during the past 133 years."

Of how and why he got in to advertising, he said: "I don't think that everything is measured by definite decisions—one day when I was suddenly going into advertising. . . . It just gradually happened. I was interested in writing. I was interested in art, and when the opportunity came along to do writing and art in advertising, I just took the opportunity."

He had an absolute aversion to the notion that advertising could be done by formula. He was very careful to make a strong distinction between philosophy, in which he trusted, and formulae, which he recognized encouraged repetitive situations.

He believed in the arcana of creativity—not just how people worked but even how to select them. In 1964, as reported by Denis Higgins in *The Art of Writing Advertising*, he was confronted by an interviewer trying to analyze just how and why he was such an original advertising thinker. Asked if there were any striking characteristics unique to talented writers and art directors, he said, "One of the problems here [in this interview] is that we're looking for a formula. What makes a good writer? It's a danger . . . I remember those old *Times* interviews where the interviewer would talk to the novelist or the short story writer and say, 'What time do you get up in the morning? What do you have for breakfast? What time do you start work? When do you stop work . . . ?' And the whole implication is that if you eat cornflakes at 6:30 and then take a walk and then take a nap and then start working and then stop at noon, you too can be a great writer. You can't be that mathematical and that precise. This business of trying to measure everything in precise terms is one of the problems with advertising today. This leads to a worship of research. We're all concerned about the facts we get and not about how provocative we can make those facts to the consumer."

To Madison Avenue of that era, fixated and engorged on facts and numbers, viewing and audience ratings, this was a heresy close to madness. But it was also music to the ears of generations of creative people who felt that all their lives their ideas, thoughts and talent, the very things they believed they were hired for, were prescribed and proscribed. And it's that sort of thinking that changed so much of advertising as then known.

1   The Story So Far

"Somewhere in this industry
this has happened before."

ROGER STERLING **MAD MEN**

It was the best of times, it was the best of times. To be white, male, and healthy in New York in the 1950s was to be as blessed as any individual at any time in history. The booming wartime economy had given way to a booming peacetime economy, fuelled by full production to meet the voracious demand from buyers nourished by the innovation and choice now available in their bounteous new "supermarkets."

One almost unbelievable statistic indicates just how the city experienced its own stampede by the business community; between 1950 and 1960 more new office space was added to New York than existed in the rest of the world at the time. In one decade that one city more than doubled the world's available office space. And all of it went upward, transforming, for example, midtown Park Avenue from a sedate backwater of domestic brownstones into a vast glistening river of glass and steel.

While Europeans still shivered, exhausted, in their damp monochrome deprivation in the aftermath of the ruinous war, New Yorkers assumed world leadership with a cool sophistication that they'd previously granted to Paris, Rome or London. In the excited, urgent chatter in the new air-conditioned offices, in the packed bars and increasingly worldly restaurants, in the crammed theater lobbies and Fifth Avenue stores there was a new confidence gained from global domination. New Yorkers basked in the health and wealth reflected back at them in the glass and chrome of their elegant, bustling streets. They revelled in their status as citizens of the busiest, noisiest, fastest growing, most advanced, most cosmopolitan, coolest, most desirable, and most photogenic city in the world.

As "the highway between those two most powerful forces known to man, supply, and demand," advertising was on the crest of a wave too. Between 1949 and 1959, total advertising spending more than doubled, from $5.21 billion to $11.27 billion. As a measure of what mattered to people, the top twelve advertisers mid decade included three car manufacturers (General Motors, Ford, and Chrysler); three hygiene and personal grooming companies (Proctor & Gamble, Colgate-Palmolive, and Lever Brothers); two food marketers (National Dairy Products, including Kraft, and General Foods); two electrical goods giants (RCA and Westinghouse—mainly producers of radios, television sets, and radiograms); and an alcohol producer (Seagram).

The money was split more or less equally among magazines, newspapers, and radio. Television wasn't a serious contender for advertising spend until later in the decade, the proportion of households with a television set rising from 10 percent in 1950 to 90 percent in 1960.

WITH THIS MASSIVE expansion in media activity, advertising came under public scrutiny more than ever, and plenty of the comment was not favorable. Arthur Schlesinger, Special Advisor to President Kennedy, had called advertising "awful." Arnold Toynbee, a British historian, complained, "I cannot think of any circumstances in which advertising would not be an evil."

Advertising's own practitioners seemed only too happy to stick the boot into the business. Nearly a dozen novels published in the fifties featured hollowed-out advertising employees, filled with self-loathing for what they did, including *Aurora Dawn*, the first novel by Herman Wouk (featuring a fictitious ad agency, Grovell & Leach—*there's* a giveaway). All but one of these novels were written by people either in, or closely allied to, the advertising business.

The Hucksters, written by copywriter Frederic Wakeman, is a typical example. The novel was filmed in 1947 with Clark Gable in the starring role of advertising executive Vic Norman, working on the Beautee Soap account. It chronicles dirty tricks, flesh-creeping client obsequiousness, and all-encompassing contempt; contempt for the consumer, for colleagues, for the advertising business, and for himself. Initially Gable didn't even want the role, describing it as "filthy and not entertainment."

Vic Norman's client is the unspeakably vulgar autocrat Evan L. Evans. He was based on George Washington Hill, the Lucky Strike client of Foote, Cone & Belding where Wakeman worked when he wrote the book. At one point, in a demonstration of his advertising philosophy, Evans spits on the conference table and says, "You've just seen me do a disgusting thing— but you'll all remember it." To make the same point Hill had once pulled out his dental bridge in front of Raymond Rubicam, his account director on the Pall Mall account. He told him this was how he amused his granddaughter, and that engaging the public was no different.

In Sloan Wilson's *The Man in the Grey Flannel Suit*, a title which for at least two decades supplied a shorthand to describe admen's dress (inaccurately, as it happened, as in the 1950s they preferred the more buttoned-down, dark-suited Wall Street look of Brooks Brothers), Gregory Peck plays Tom Rath, a PR man and mentally scarred World War II veteran who leaves a job in the charity sector to work for a TV network. Increasingly disillusioned with the job, the politics, the surrounding inertia, and the suspect morality, Rath leaves the business to lead a less pressured, more family-centered life.

ADVERTISING WAS ALSO fair game for a kicking as screenwriters jogged by on their way to bigger themes. In the 1957 Sidney Lumet film *Twelve Angry Men*, the cheesily handsome juror who seems least in touch with reality and most prepared to change his mind just had to be in advertising; even in lighthearted mode, the husband in the long-running early sixties TV series *Bewitched* was a permanently bewildered advertising executive, with an obsequious client-pleasing boss, while the romantic romp *Lover Come Back* sees Doris Day trying to get even with rival agency head Rock Hudson for his unethical tactics in stealing a client.

Elements of these portrayals must have been true. Certainly, advertising was wearing and mentally draining; apart from anything else, ad men

Here's how <u>your</u> family will find out...

IT PAYS
TO OWN A DODGE

Let's say your family is the kind that wants more than you get in the "low-priced" field. You want more room and comfort. You want more solidness on the road. You want a car that's truly fine in its deep-down quality. And most of all, you want a car you can all enjoy without going "overboard" on purchase price, or on gas and upkeep costs.

So head for your Dodge dealer's—and find a revelation!

The savings start right off the bat! You find that a big, solid Dodge Coronet *costs less to buy* than any car that comes close to it in comfort, roominess, fine-car looks and handling. It pays you $100, $200 or *more* to choose Dodge over comparable models of other cars in the field. Matter of fact, your Dodge may cost you less than smaller, less substantial models in the low-priced field.

You'll notice the difference in gas bills! In the recent Mobilgas Economy Run, a Dodge V-8 delivered an outstanding 21.74 miles per gallon. Dodge not only finished 1-2 in the low-medium price field, it also topped all other cars from the low-price V-8 field on up. In many other ways—tune-up costs, brake lining wear, spark plug replacement—a Dodge *costs less to drive.*

Your vacation—the "Big Pay-off!" On top of your savings on purchase price, gas economy, upkeep costs—you'll discover how much *more* you get in Dodge. More room, more comfort. The road-hugging miracle of Torsion-Aire Ride; the security of Total-Contact Brakes and Safety-Rim Wheels— all at no extra cost. It's just *more* car for the money.

Winner in this year's Mobilgas Economy Run '59 DODGE
A DIVISION OF CHRYSLER CORPORATION

ABOVE *Acres of crunchy gravel, miles of smiles; there was the real world and there was the world of auto advertising.*

worked extraordinarily long hours, often with detrimental effect on their health; an *Advertising Age* survey reported in 1956 that senior advertising executives died at an average age of 57.9, ten years under the national average. In addition, the unpredictable nature of the business generated constant anxiety over client loss and the immediate brutal consequences. In return, the rewards were high, with admen earning anything up to 50 percent more than their equivalents in other businesses. But that of course is a double-edged sword: the more you're paid, the more you have to lose. "Ulcer Gulch" became a sardonic way of referring to Madison Avenue.

The fabled expense account lifestyle, too, was often anything but glitzy for the agency man. It wasn't always a boozy lunch or night with his friends and colleagues from around the business. This genuinely was the era of the three-martini lunch and five-course dinner, and the ad executive ate and drank them whether he wanted to or not. It all depended on the client, who frequently viewed a trip to his agency as light relief from what was often a humdrum life somewhere in middle-America, far from the bright lights of the most fabulous city on earth.

He could look forward to a couple of days in a swanky New York hotel, a visit to the agency with the opportunity from reception onward to ogle some fine legs and even finer busts. There would be a well-catered meeting in the agency's sumptuous conference room, maybe enlivened by the presence of some of the menagerie otherwise known as the creative department, in which he could beat up or lift up the agency depending on his mood. Business out of the way, there'd be a big lunch at Nino's or Rattazzi's—where the standard martini glass was eight ounces—followed by an afternoon spent shopping, then cocktails with the agency at the Algonquin, a show, and dinner at 21 or Copacabana. Then a club—perhaps a clip joint—before heading back to the Midwest or the South the next day, and all without so much as a glimpse of a bill at any time, day or night.

Great for the client once in a while—but four days a week for the account men with their fixed smiles, ready jokes, and the ever open wallet, it was liver-destroying purgatory.

Obsequiousness and double dealing are sadly inevitable in an unregulated service industry, and advertising was never going to be an exception—at least until the end of the fifties. Unprotected by guilds or freemasonry or professional codes, it was still a free-for-all less than sixty years from its raw-boned frontier days as a media broking business.

AS AN INDUSTRY, advertising had waxed and waned with national events. Its first great boom came after the Civil War, another was induced by World War I; helplessly tied to the market it slumped in the Depression, then picked up with the growth of mass production and greater availability of goods. The subsequent introduction of self-service, when the housewife could no longer necessarily take advice and comfort in the words of the storekeeper as her personal shopper, created a demand for more paid-for public advocacy. Which is as good a definition of advertising as any.

Early advertising agencies in the 1800s simply sold space in newspapers to advertisers, buying column inches from the publishers either directly for their customers or for themselves to sell later on. Few, if any, rate cards were published, and ignorance abounded—ignorance of the true prices, value, readership, reach, influence, even of how many newspapers there actually were.

What made it even more unruly was the fact that while the agencies charged their customers a commission, they also regularly took kickbacks from the newspapers, or at best didn't pass on discounted rates. From their point of view it wasn't so much a conflict as a confluence of interest. While ostensibly acting in pursuit of a better deal for their customers, it was clearly to their advantage to spend as much as they could of their customers' money; the customer-derived commission, based on a percentage, was higher, and their "reward" from a grateful newspaper was greater. What appeared on the space the agencies were broking was none of their business—the actual content of the ads was usually supplied by their customer.

But gradually, order emerged from the chaos as common and business sense combined to bring clarity to the practice. In Philadelphia, in 1869, George P. Rowell brought out the first ever comprehensive guide to media rates. Rowell's *American Newspaper Dictionary* enabled a client to plan and buy their media from a substantial choice of publication styles, locations, and readership profiles. It included circulation figures, and the immediate availability of such information undermined the hucksterish behavior of the contemporary advertising agencies. Worse for them, such transparency threatened their very existence as a client could now do for himself what he'd previously needed their "insider knowledge" and "expertise" to achieve.

To survive the agencies had to offer more, and this took the form of creative services—advice on how to prepare and write the ads. They would charge for the space plus the costs of creating the ad, and thus the model for the advertising agency of the twentieth century—an organization that will advise you on not just where to place your advertisements but what to say in them, and then produce those ads—was created.

It would contain media specialists, creative people (both writers and artists), and account managers or executives to liaise between the clients and the agency staff. Those early agencies employed quite a few of their copywriters from a field force of freelancers that had grown up working directly for clients. They cut their teeth on retail store advertising, some toiletries and hardware products, and particularly patent medicines—quack remedies sold in vast numbers throughout the United States.

The market for these remedies was huge, partly assured by the fact that many of the potions included alcohol or even opium, a legitimate way around temperance for those who were pious enough to be claiming abstention. The inventiveness of the manufacturers and the copywriters in coming up with increasingly vague scary diseases and afflictions that only they could fix was unbounded, preying on the fears of a simply-educated and gullible public. And the margins on these potions, which were often, apart from the alcohol, little more than colored water, were so vast that the producers could afford to spend large sums on promoting their products. They had found that the reassurance and promised salvation in the advertised testimonials from "doctors" and the "cured" proved highly effective. As Stephen Fox reports in *The Mirror Makers*, one such patent medicine proprietor claimed, "I can advertise dishwater and sell it, just as well as an article of merit. It's all in the advertising." It's hardly surprising that, with ethics like that, and with the reputation it had gained in its early days, advertising was still seen as a far from respectable activity.

HOWEVER, THE INDUSTRY was maturing, though that was not always driven by the agencies. In 1892, the *Ladies' Home Journal* had banned patent medicine ads, and growing organizations like P&G and Kellogg took pride in their probity. They were selling wholesome products for wholesome families and they simply would not tolerate suppliers of ill-repute. So by the 1950s many agencies were fiercely honorable, renowned for watertight integrity, J Walter Thompson (JWT) being a prominent example. In 1955, Jeremy Bullmore, a young copywriter from JWT London was sent to the New York office to learn about making TV commercials—in the run up to their first appearances on UK television in 1955 no one there had any idea how to write or make them. Before he left for the fourteen-hour flight, the only advice he was given by his boss was "get your hair cut and don't wear suede shoes." Apparently the British thought that, to New Yorkers, suede shoes were a sign of gayness.

He found the Lexington Avenue office in the Graybar Building an austere place, far from the image of *Mad Men*'s Sterling Cooper.

"There were a lot of very serious account people, all highly intelligent but serious; they were grown-up, they didn't have a lot of fun. They were very well-educated but it was much more like an agreeable law firm, not an agency. Nobody questioned the fact that you were there to use your brains on your client's behalf, that absolutely didn't need to be said. They took the business very seriously; I mean it, I'm not sure the word creative was used at all. There was the art department and the editorial department, which was the copy department, showing its origins in journalism. And the lady copywriters sat in their own compounds, wearing hats."

Hats seem to have been big, particularly with the women at JWT. Wally O'Brien, an account man, recalls the midweek queue outside the New England Room (a boardroom that resembled the kitchen of a New England farmhouse, a JWT feature dating back to pre-war days). "Wednesday was 'Women's Day,' when only women could eat in the room, and they'd vie with each other to wear the most outrageous hat to lunch. We'd stand outside to see them go past on their way in!"

The agency wouldn't accept an alcohol or cigarette account and they'd never pitch for new business competitively or speculatively, on the argument that they couldn't put forward responsible recommendations until they had a real, deep understanding of the client's market.

Alcohol consumption in the office was almost unheard of. And ever since *Reader's Digest* published its 1952 "Cancer by the Carton" article, examining possible links between tobacco and cancer (long before the 1964 Surgeon General's report on the effects of smoking on health), several agencies refused to handle tobacco, extraordinarily lucrative though it was. Several prominent figures called for it to be banned and plenty more dropped it on the announcement, including both Bill Bernbach and David Ogilvy. Indeed, the head of McCann-Erickson, Emerson Foote, resigned because his agency continued to handle cigarettes.

So the business wasn't without its principles and principled people. Nevertheless, the novelists were right in their portrayal of a group of people who, rightly or wrongly, were riddled with low self-esteem. Reported in a lengthy essay in *Time* magazine, late in 1962, only 8 percent of admen polled believed that their fellow admen were "honest." Indeed, so much self-examination and self-flagellation was going on that the president of the American Association of Advertising Agencies urged his members to stop "staring into the mirror to count the pimples, broken veins, and wattles on the serene, handsome, and competent face we hope to present to the public."

IN 1957, one book, Vance Packard's *The Hidden Persuaders* probably did more damage to the reputation of advertising than any other single tangible factor. It claimed to expose practices within the advertising business of subconscious coercion, subliminal advertising, and wonderful and weird techniques that either forced us to surrender our innermost thoughts, fears, and desires, or got us all buying products without ever realizing why we were doing it.

Clearly a sensation-seeking writer—*Time* magazine in 1962 described Packard as "one of the nation's most talented self-advertisers"—his book promoted the discomfiting notions, wheezes, and theories of the quack psychologists and pointy-bearded analysts who were besieging agencies with quick-fix nostrums derived from consumer motivational research, depth psychology, and other psychological techniques.

To be fair to Packard, these people and their ideas (among them Ernest Dichter, a Viennese psychologist with a Freudian-based résumé, who set up shop in a Manhattan suburb to promote his newly created "science" of motivational research) did exist, and in trying to get business from clients and agencies they probably were making the claims he reported. But that doesn't mean they were actually being implemented, let alone the least bit effective or successful. As most people who have ever worked in an agency for any length of time will tell you, it's far more a matter of intuitive trial and error than finely tuned science.

Yet the book, perhaps preying on the paranoia of a fearful nation, engaged in the Cold War and fed fanciful science-fiction tales of invisible rays and undetectable brainwashing, was a bestseller for six months, exercising almost supernatural power over its readers. In 1966, Victor Navasky, now a professor at the Columbia University Graduate School of Journalism, wrote for *The New York Times*: "In the thirties, economists knocked advertising. In the forties, novelists knocked advertising. In the fifties, sociologists knocked advertising and Hollywood began making movies out of the novels of the forties. In the sixties, the politicians who saw the movies began to attack advertising. . . . It has been attacked for 'arousing anxieties and manipulating the fears of consumers to coerce them into buying' and at the same time it has been dismissed as impotent, misdirected, and irrelevant."

The final nail? Some time in the mid fifties, Webster's dictionary changed it's definition of "huckster" from simply "hawker, peddler" to add "one who produces promotional material for commercial clients, particularly radio and newspapers." The humiliation was complete.

The real cause of discontent, both internal and external, was the advertising itself. By and large, it was execrable. To make matters worse, the more the economy boomed, the more there was of it to see.

A 1962 *Time* article stated, "Many admen tend to ascribe much of the responsibility for television's excesses to one source: Manhattan's Ted Bates & Co, which funnels a greater percentage of its business into TV than any other agency (80 percent) and has rocketed from nowhere in 1940 to fifth place among all US agencies. . . . The enfant terrible at Bates is Chairman Rosser Reeves, fifty-two, who propagated the dogma of the Unique Selling Proposition, or USP. The rule: find a unique proposition that promises a specific benefit to the customer and will thereby sell The Product . . . the agency hammers it home with water torture repetition."

IF, FOR GENERATIONS OF CREATIVE people, Bill Bernbach is their Redeemer, no one more than Rosser Reeves best personifies the antiChrist. By his invention and implementation of the USP, Reeves probably had as huge an influence on the course of advertising as his contemporary, but in the diametrically opposite direction.

Actually, the problem so many ad people had with Reeves was not so much the USP itself, it was the way he went about implementing it and his utter indifference to the wider effect of his advertising on the public.

One of his most notorious commercials was for Anacin: hammers banging away at the inside of a cartoon head. It ran unchanged for seven years and when you'd seen it once you never needed or wanted to see it ever again. That it must have cured millions of headaches there can be little doubt, as sales tripled and the advert made more money for Reeves' client, as he liked to point out, than *Gone with the Wind*, on a production budget of just $8,200. The media spend over that period was $86,400,000, a staggering amount for the era. The question that never bothered him was how many headaches it, and so many others of his commercials, caused.

A story he liked to tell clients says it all. A farmer buys a mule that he finds to be unusually stubborn and simply won't get going. He takes it to an old farmhand who is said to know everything there is to know about mules. For $5 he says he can fix it. The money changes hands and the old man picks up a 45-pound hammer and hits the mule as hard as he can, right between the ears.

"Hey," says the owner, "I paid you to cure him, not kill him!"

"I know," says the old man, "but first I have to get his attention."

Hit them hard, straight between the ears, painfully, mercilessly—and keep hitting them until they give in. Boring, repetitive commercials, usually featuring quasi-scientists in white coats or basic graphic devices with a voice-over slamming home a product virtue—over and over again: "Four out of five doctors . . ."

Typical of this "monkey see, monkey do" approach was a commercial for M&Ms, focusing on the utilitarian point that the candy doesn't melt in the hand. Two closed fists were shown, the viewer asked to guess which hand holds the M&Ms. Then they're opened and one is messy, and a grinning presenter helps us to the desired conclusion.

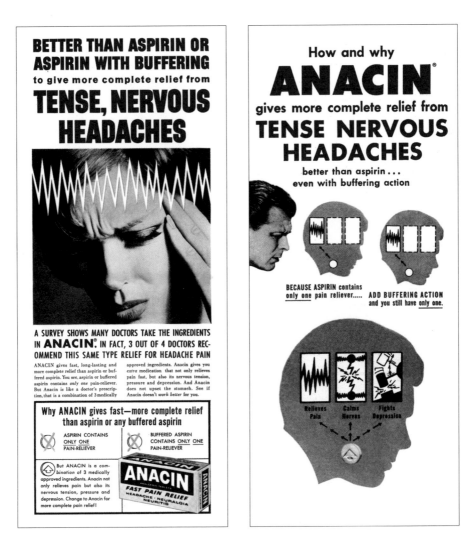

The same 1962 *Time* article continued, "the average American is now exposed to ten thousand TV commercials a year. As the number increases, so do the admen's worries about 'overexposure.'"

There had been plenty of opportunity for overexposure before, in the heyday of radio. But the new intrusiveness of television, which demanded (and got) both ears and eyes, together with the repetitiveness of the new thirty-second TV commercial format meant that "most admen profess to detect evidence of . . . more vocal public irritation with strident or tasteless ads."

Even more uncompromising, Fairfax Cone, his own agency a big TV spender, said to the Federal Communications Commission, "The great mass of television viewers are treated to an almost continuous program of tastelessness, which is projected on behalf of competitive products of little interest and only occasional necessity."

Bear in mind, this was before the remote control and there was no way of changing channel or switching off without actually getting off the couch and walking to the set. Norman Strouse, then president of JWT, worried, "It is a simple matter to turn a page but TV makes it possible for advertisers to impose rudely on the viewer with every unhappy practice of the industry—hard sell, bad taste, driving repetition." And the more they saw of it, the more the public disliked it.

YET REEVES HIMSELF was the polar opposite of the crude salesman and media hooligan that his legacy would suggest. Born in 1910, he was the son of a Virginian minister and a graduate of the University of Virginia. It seems he viewed advertising simply as an activity to make money to enrich his leisure time, and his leisure time was as cultured as his output was uncouth. It was as if there were two Reeves.

Living in Greenwich Village during the beatnik era, he was a poet, a novelist, a keen racing yachtsman and pilot, and, testament to tremendous concentration and analytical powers, captain of the 1955 US chess team picked to play Russia. He was good company, quick-witted, and whilst normally showing a calm poise, he also occasionally betrayed a disarming enthusiasm once he got his teeth into something. His interests even extended to being part of a consortium of eleven Southern businessmen,

"What do you want out of me? Fine writing? Do you want masterpieces? Do you want glowing things that can be framed by copywriters? Or do you want to see the goddam sales curve stop moving down and start moving up?"

ROSSER REEVES

mainly Brown and Williamson tobacco executives, who "owned" Cassius Clay (later Muhammad Ali) in the early days of his career.

A huge believer in research and analysis, he passionately held that entertainment or charm in advertising were not just unnecessary but undesirable, describing them as "video vampires." And any departure from an agreed proposition, even in a small detail, was to be avoided.

In 1961, Reeves' philosophy, and guidance on its implementation, was collated into his book *Reality in Advertising*, which was originally written as a document for executives joining the agency, releasing a torrent of imitative commercials—repetitive, didactic, fact-rich, and entertainment-poor. Uncertain clients, finding reassurance in text books that gave "theories" of advertising a quasi-academic respectability, and looking for risk-free creative "solutions," embraced the technique. And as so much TV advertising around the world was for companies exclusively led from the United States, it quickly became the style of the first advertising that most of the world would experience on their televisions. Any criticism of his methods would have been robustly kicked into the long grass.

"Getting the message into the most people at the lowest possible cost, well, it's almost a problem in engineering, and we should subordinate our own creative impulses to that one overall objective. Does this advertisement move an idea from the inside of my head to the inside of the public's head? The most people at the lowest possible cost? What else is this business about? . . . It's a technical job."

Reeves had a point; Bates was almost exclusively a packaged goods agency and despite the antipathy it created, not just for its own sake but for all advertising, clearly a lot of the time his utilitarian advertising for those low cost, functional products was effective. Companies like

P&G adopted it as the only way in which they wanted their advertising to be conducted.

This was the era of constant product innovation, when new variations of medicines, shaving products, hair shampoos, skin creams or foods were flooding the market, to the potential bewilderment of the public. It's easy to understand that advertising, which was little more than a shouted bulletin board, was often the most efficient way to elevate your pitch above the daily cacophony. And its charisma-free directness was the quickest way to explain the benefits of, say, the previously unheard of product now being sold as hair conditioner.

But many inside advertising would argue that this soulless hard-sell approach was working for its advertisers at the expense of advertising as a whole. This certainly was not the era when the consumer would claim to prefer the commercials to the programs.

It took the likes of Reeves' even more famous brother-in-law, not always one of his greatest fans, to both lighten and soften the advertising mood.

2 A Growing Respect

"Ogilvy wrote a book. I got the galleys. . . . Advertising's already up there with lawyers as the most reviled. This is not going to help."

ROGER STERLING MAD MEN

David Ogilvy married Rosser Reeves' wife's sister in 1939. By several measures the two men were similar: workaholics, strongly opinionated advertising writers, and both, in their demeanor at least, cultivated men. But while for Reeves culture ended at his typewriter keys, Ogilvy carried all his considerable personal style into his and his eponymous agency's work. From the early-fifties onward, a stream of articulate and elegantly art-directed print campaigns issued from Ogilvy, Benson & Mather (OB&M), all assuming literacy and sophistication on the part of the reader—and usually offering the promise of yet more sophistication through the use of the product they were advertising.

Ogilvy was English, at a time when an English accent was still rare and hugely prized in New York. Ogilvy's was a particularly well-modulated accent, and with his long, lean figure, foppish hair, and ever present pipe, he was every bit Hollywood's idea of the perfect English gentleman, a character he exploited fully.

Ken Roman, his biographer, who worked with Ogilvy and knew him closely from 1963 until he died in 1999, says, "He dressed for his parts. He didn't wear a business suit. Sometimes he dressed as the English country gentleman with his brogues, a tweed jacket, and lapels on his vest. Sometimes he wore a kilt, before anyone had seen one. Sometimes, at big state occasions, he put on this kind of a purple vest that looked vaguely ecclesiastical. But he never wore a normal business suit, never."

Ogilvy's route to fame and fortune in New York was as peripatetic as it was exotic. Born in England in 1911, he won a scholarship to study history at Christ Church College, Oxford. He left without completing his degree, having suffered some sort of block, and, as quoted by Bart Cummings in *The Benevolent Dictators*, "ran away from the cultured, civilized life, and changed class and tried to become a workman. I went to Paris and got a job as a chef in the great kitchen at the Hotel Majestic." He withstood the "slave wages, fiendish pressure, and perpetual exhaustion" for a year, returned to England, and began selling Aga cookers door to door. His sales prowess brought him to the attention of his elder brother Francis's employers at the advertising agency Mather & Crowther (M&C).

Ogilvy accepted the offer of a job as an account executive and did well, but felt he was working in his brother's shadow. To prove his independence he asked for a transfer to M&C's US office. He went to New York in 1938, and by the end of a year he loved it so much he didn't think of returning to England. With no firm intention of continuing with a career in advertising, he drifted into his next job, but it turned out to be critical in the formulation of his theories and future practices. He joined George Gallup's company and entered the new but rapidly expanding world of consumer research.

ADVERTISING RESEARCH had existed since the late nineteenth century in the form of crude testing of different versions of ads by evaluating coupon responses. Mail order shopping was dominant in a dissipated, still largely rural population, so it was easy to measure the success of an ad simply by tracking the volume of orders that followed each insertion. The offer of a free sample at the bottom of an advert for a new beauty soap wasn't generosity on the part of the manufacturer, nor was it just about getting a trial; it elicited a coupon to be returned to the company. The coupons were coded to identify the specific advert and the publication in which it had appeared, and by analysis of the returned coupons a basic picture could be drawn of which version of the ads, running in which publications, were the most successful.

But the research was rough and ready and reactive; it could only give you a crude view afterwards, which you could then apply to your next insertion. As the development of mass production and branded products fed the growth of advertising, market research slowly grew up alongside it, developing from "How did we do?" to "Why?" to "How can we do it better?"

In an attempt to assuage the advertisers' anxiety—best expressed by the nineteenth-century Philadelphia store owner John Wannamaker when he said, "Half the money I spend on advertising is wasted; the trouble is I don't know which half"—agencies racheted up their research presentations, claiming to be able to produce super-efficient advertising based on their "proprietary" research techniques.

BY THE 1930S, research had become the Holy Grail of advertising; clients, often uncertain and uncomfortable when handling and evaluating abstract "creative" ideas, were much happier pouring over the endless charts and graphs churned out by the research people, and were reassured by the rules guiding them through the alien world of advertising creativity. The copywriter's imagination and individuality was allowed to run only to the point at which it interfered with the "proven" rules of how they should do their ads, and intuition became subordinated to research reports.

An audience measurement system was developed by Claude Hooper, specifically to cater for the explosive interest in radio as an advertising medium, and the phrase "Hooper Ratings" became the scourge of radio producers and agencies across the country. Such was the client confidence in their research that a low Hooper rating on a Monday morning could break a Saturday night radio show.

In 1931 George Gallup, then a professor of journalism at Northwestern, produced a report of his research into readers' reactions to advertisements in magazines. He found that ads based around sex and vanity were the most popular with women, the second most popular being those based on the quality of the product. Men also ranked those as their top two, only in reverse order. But in the same survey, Gallup found that those approaches were the two least favored by advertisers, who preferred ads leading on efficiency and economy—which were the least favored by all readers.

ABOVE *Brothers-in-law but in little else;*
David Ogilvy (left) and Rosser Reeves
(right).

The impact of his findings attracted major attention across the advertising world and he was wooed by several of the larger agencies. He eventually joined Young & Rubicam (Y&R) to head their research department and then in 1935 set up the American Institute of Public Opinion, which later became The Gallup Organization. The main purpose was the objective measurement of what "the people" were thinking, and his first big success was the correct forecasting of the 1936 election, Roosevelt's victory over Landon. The Literary Digest, the respected pollster of the day, had projected a Landon landslide. High on the success, Gallup's business expanded—and it was this organization that David Ogilvy joined in 1939.

IN THE THREE YEARS he was with Gallup, Ogilvy conducted more than four hundred surveys, many of them in Hollywood, pre-testing films. Interrogating the US public on how they perceive and receive communications designed to entertain them was clearly ideal grounding for a future career in advertising. The rigor of the research and analysis also influenced the development of what became his highly disciplined and well-documented philosophy of advertising.

By the time Ogilvy returned to New York, now aged thirty-eight, he'd convinced himself he wanted to be a copywriter but felt no one would employ him as he'd never done the job formally. The only other route open to him was to start his own agency. His personal wealth amounted to $6,000 but his brother persuaded his old British agency M&C, together with another London agency, SH Benson, to invest in the venture on condition he employed an American partner—they felt a British man in New York wouldn't have the business credibility. So in 1948 he set up Hewitt, Ogilvy, Benson & Mather with Anderson Hewitt, a Chicago advertising executive who contributed $14,000. Hewitt left the company five years later, when it became Ogilvy, Benson & Mather.

Their first piece of business was Wedgwood, the china manufacturer. It's a typical Ogilvy product, reflecting a genteel refinement. Indeed, his earliest successes were for similar "drawing room" type products. And despite their small size, they could well be described as his biggest triumphs, since they're still amongst the most famous work his agency ever did and on which the agency was initially built.

Elegant literary copy and captivating photographs selling the historical and cultural benefits of a holiday in Britain for the British Tourist Association was an early noted campaign. Ogilvy said he was happiest working on products that interested him and they tended to be products with a touch of class, more white than blue collar. In fact, often he couldn't help imbuing the one with the status of the other, as in an ad for Austin cars with the headline attributed to an anonymous diplomat, "I'm sending my son to Groton with the money I've saved driving an Austin." In Ogilvy's velvet-cushioned world, a cheap car was sold not on the basis of anything as sordid as thrift or value but on the promise of a posh education for the children of the diplomatic classes.

It was entirely consistent that he should describe the account executives he wanted as the backbone of his agency as "gentlemen with brains."

HATHAWAY WAS a medium-priced range of shirts from a small Maine clothing manufacturer with an advertising budget of just $30,000. Typically, Ogilvy decided that the shirts would be modeled on a man of some sort of distinction and they settled on a dispossessed White Russian baron turned part-time PR man, George Wrangell. He definitely had the aristocratic look but was often in poor health and, according to Cliff Field who wrote a lot of the ads over the ten-year period, "a difficult man to photograph. He had a tendency to turn blue outdoors."

For no clear reason other than he had been intrigued by a picture of Lewis Douglas (the US Ambassador to Britain) wearing a patch over one eye after a fishing accident, on the morning of the shoot Ogilvy bought a handful of eyepatches. At the shoot, he asked that Wrangell be photographed with and without one of the eyepatches, and in the end he chose a version with the patch.

The first ad ran in *The New Yorker* on September 22, 1951. It was an instant success. The device had exactly the effect Ogilvy wanted, adding intrigue and narrative as a background to the shirts. The campaign developed, showing Wrangell engaged in all sorts of narrative-rich situations; as a painter, an orchestral conductor, a classical musician— always with the eyepatch. Soon it became a popular prop at parties and offices, and other campaigns aped it, even putting it on animals. To

Hathaway imports Ponja cloth—from London

IN THIS PHOTOGRAPH Baron Wrangell is wearing what is probably the
lightest shirt Hathaway ever made. So
light, says the Baron, that at one point he
began to wonder whether he had forgot-
ten to put it on.

The original Ponja cloth came from
India, but it is now woven in Britain. The
patterns are hand-printed by the illustrious
Aldwinckle in London, using a process
which is more than a hundred years old.
These classic patterns are called *foulards*,
and they are also used for the most sought-
after English neckties.

The shirt in our photograph comes in a
wide range of different colors—all in the
impeccable tradition of English taste. The
tailoring is on the loose side—very comfortable and informal. You can wear the
shirt open or closed at the neck, and it is
cut to be worn either inside your trousers
or outside. The price is $10.95. At the
most distinguished stores, or write C. F.
Hathaway, Waterville, Maine.

ABOVE *Never underestimate the power of an
eyepatch; one example of the Hathaway campaign.*
OPPOSITE *An Ogilvy campaign? Look again—these
are actually four completely different campaigns for
(clockwise from top left) Viyella, Hathaway, British
Tourist Board, and Schweppes.*

See The Conquering Hero Comes—in a Viyella® Robe!

Sound the trumpets, beat the drums, see the conquering hero comes—dressed to the nines in a Viyella robe, and armed with Sunday breakfast for his deserving bride. The superb thing about a Viyella bathrobe is that you can wash it. If it shrinks, we replace. Lamby-soft Viyella (rhymes with hi-ella) wears for years. A customer who bought a Viyella bathrobe ten years ago tells us that he has had it washed and cleaned more than sixty times. "The colors are just as bright and distinct as when it was new . . . the only casualty throughout the years has been the loss of two buttons." Viyella robes (like the one our hero is wearing) come in authentic tartans, naturally, checks, stripes and plain colors. They weigh only 21 ounces and can be packed in your brief case next time you travel. $18.50 at fine stores everywhere. For the name of your nearest retailer write William Hollins & Company, Inc., 347 Madison Avenue, New York 17, New York. MU 4-7330.

This shirt has an unusual collar. Hathaway has removed one layer of its lining—so that your neck can breathe.

Hathaway reveals the truth about men who wear drip-dry shirts

We have discovered that many men who swear by Hathaway's drip-dry shirts never drip them dry. They cheerfully send them to the laundry, just like any other shirt.

We asked some of these men why on earth they buy our drip-dry shirts in preference to our others. And their answers boil down to this:

After a hard day, a Hathaway drip-dry looks neater than any other shirt known to man. It is virtually crease-proof.

Of course, if you ever wash one of these Hathaway shirts yourself, you can trust it to drip-dry looking as crisp as if you'd ironed it.

The sea-blue shirt in our picture is a summer blend of Dacron polyester fiber and cotton. It weighs a scant five ounces, and also comes in white and the subdued shades at the right: Sahara, Cactus, and Scotch Dawn. About $7.50.

Dacron is a Du Pont trademark.

For the names of stores, write to C. F. Hathaway, Waterville, Maine. Or call OXford 7-5566 in New York.

She's got two more cases of Schweppes Bitter Lemon stashed away in the trunk.

Is it cricket to hoard new Schweppes **Bitter Lemon**?

(No—but it's smart. Last year Schweppes almost ran out of the stuff.)

You are looking at a *practical* girl. Last year, during the Bitter Lemon drought, even Commander Whitehead could have saved her only a six-pack.

This year, she isn't taking chances. As you can see above, she's hoarding cases of Schweppes Bitter Lemon.

Bitter Lemon is the newest triumph of the House of Schweppes. It was an immediate sensation in England. In America, connoisseurs are drinking it as if there were no tomorrow.

Schweppes Bitter Lemon is a great mixer. You'll get a remarkably good drink when you mix it with gin, vodka, bourbon, rum—you name it. Schweppes Bitter Lemon is also the first *adult* soft drink. It has a tart, lemony taste. So sophisticated that it's the only soft drink children don't like. All the more for you.

The extraordinary demand for Schweppes Bitter Lemon goes on and on. So rush to your store now!

Caution: To get the real thing—make sure the label on every bottle reads "*Schweppes Bitter Lemon.*"

Henry VII, Elizabeth I and Mary Queen of Scots are buried in this chapel.

Tread softly past the long, long sleep of kings

This is Henry VII's chapel in Westminster Abbey. These windows have filtered the sunlight of five centuries. They have also seen the crowning of twenty-two kings.

Three monarchs rest here now. Henry, Elizabeth and Mary. Such are their names in sleep. No titles. No trumpets. The banners hang battle-heavy and becalmed. But still the royal crown remains. *Honi soit qui mal y pense.*

When you go to Britain, make yourself this promise. Visit at least one of the thirty great cathedrals. Their famous names thunder! Durham and Armagh. Or they chime! Lincoln and Canterbury. And sometimes they whisper. Winchester, Norwich, Salisbury and Wells. Get a map and make your choice.

Each cathedral transcends the noblest single work of art. It is a pinnacle of faith and an act of centuries. It is an offering of human hands as close to Abraham as it is to Bach. Listen to the soaring choirs at evensong. And, if you can, go at Christmas or Easter. You will rejoice that you did.

For free illustrated literature, see your travel agent or write Box 100, British Travel Association.

In New York—680 Fifth Ave.; In Los Angeles—612 So. Flower St.; In Chicago—39 So. LaSalle St.; In Canada—151 Bloor St. West, Toronto.

maintain an upmarket image the ads ran only in the smart, literary *New Yorker*, the magazine's ad manager saying he'd never seen such interest in a campaign.

Between 1950 and 1969, Hathaway sales rose from $2 million per year to $30 million; name recognition went from under 1 percent to 40 percent in ten years; and the number of stores stocking the range rose from 450 to 2,500 between 1950 and 1962.

It worked for the agency too, pulling in enquiries from such establishment clients as P&G. So recognizable and so far down the line of OB&M history did the campaign reach that, when Ogilvy's book *Confessions of an Advertising Man* came out in 1965, the publisher's sales force wore eyepatches while selling it in to stores. As an O&M executive apparently said more than thirty years after the campaign first ran, reflecting on its influence on the agency's fame and history, "We'll all have eyepatches on our tombstones."

THE NEXT MAJOR SUCCESS was the tonic water company Schweppes, a tiny piece of business that spent no more than $15,000 on their advertising. Initially, Ogilvy prepared a workmanlike campaign announcing the availability of the tonic water in the New York area, but the client wanted something more exotic. It's unclear who first made the suggestion, but the decision was made to use Commander Edward Whitehead, a former World War II Royal Navy officer who was by that time running Schweppes in the United States.

There was no doubt that he looked the part of a British naval officer ; a huge bushy beard under a large-whiskered handlebar moustache gave him a sort of camp King George V look, although what that had to do with selling tonic water is obscure. But no matter; for reasons as impenetrable as the success of the Hathaway Shirt Man, the Schweppes Tonic Man became as big a hit. For eyepatch, substitute beard.

Not that it was all plain sailing with Commander Teddy Whitehead. David Herzbrun, a creative director on the business in 1964, recalls in his book *Playing with Traffic on Madison Avenue* that Whitehead froze in front of the camera. When Harry Hamburg, the photographer, asked for a smile, what he got was "a ghastly rictus of death." Hamburg muttered to

Herzbrun that the only thing Englishmen of Whitehead's class ever thought was funny was bathroom humor.

"He got Teddy arranged in the right pose, got his camera ready and called out to the Commander, 'Say shit!'

"Whitehead said it shyly, with a rather endearing schoolboy smile.

"'Louder,' Harry commanded.

"'Shit!' roared Teddy and laughed until the tears came.

"For the next three days Harry shot as Whitehead shat; and the word never failed to produce the desired results."

As with Hathaway, the media schedule was limited, again majoring on *The New Yorker* but also including *Sports Illustrated*. Although partly driven by the limitation of the budget, it was nevertheless courageous thinking—few advertisers back then had the faith to put all their eggs in one basket. But as Whitehead said, he and Ogilvy agreed that "what the discriminating do today, the undiscriminating will do tomorrow."

It was, as they say, trucks through the night for Schweppes. The public lapped up the images of Commander Whitehead going about his high-octane life, stepping off jet planes, sporting ice on his beard at some chic ski resort, dining with a beautiful woman at a stylish restaurant. Sales were up from under a million bottles to 32 million per year in five years, a remarkable result since it had barely been heard of in the United States before.

OGILVY WAS, if not exactly a snob, certainly class conscious. As he rather characteristically put it, "There are very few products that do not benefit from being given a first-class ticket through life." Maybe it was the often experienced reaction of the Englishman of that era in New York, where in the face of the brash, loud, busy new world he retreats into a caricature of his real self and becomes even more English, brittle, and refined. It is not hostility to the surroundings, but perhaps it is to preserve the independence and objectivity of the view that first so captivated him.

He was also capable of the most breathtaking vanity, happy to be quoted by Ken Roman in such conceits as "By twenty-five I was brilliant," "I lit a candle which is still burning forty years later," and "I love reading in the press what a great copywriter I am." Ken also recalls one of the most

The man from Schweppes is here

Meet Commander Edward Whitehead, Schweppesman Extraordinary from London, England, where the house of Schweppes has been a great institution since 1794.

Commander Whitehead has come to these United States to make sure that every drop of Schweppes Quinine Water bottled here has the original flavor which has long made Schweppes the *only* mixer for an *authentic* Gin-and-Tonic.

He imports the original Schweppes elixir, and the secret of Schweppes unique carbonation is locked in his brief case. "Schweppervescence," says the Commander, *"lasts the whole drink through."*

It took Schweppes almost a hundred years to bring the flavor of their Quinine Water to its present bittersweet perfection. But it will take you only thirty seconds to mix it with ice and gin in a highball glass. *Then,* gentle reader, you will bless the day you read these words.

P.S. If your favorite store or bar doesn't yet have Schweppes, drop a card to us and we'll make the proper arrangements. Address Schweppes, 30 East 60th Street, New York City.

ABOVE AND OPPOSITE *A genuine client with a genuine beard. Commander Whitehead of Schweppes.*

SCHWEPPES DISCOVERS AMERICA—AND VICE VERSA

Piutes greet Big Chief Tonic Water from over the seas!

ABOVE, demonstrating the virtues of the original and authentic Schweppes Tonic to a group of original and authentic Americans, you see Commander Edward Whitehead—heap big chief of the whole Schweppes setup in America.

The Commander first arrived on our shores eight years ago—and you can see the results of his work all around you.

Today, there's hardly a living, breathing American who doesn't know that Schweppes is the only mixer for a *real* Gin-and-Tonic. Who hasn't tasted Schweppervescence—exuberant little bubbles that last your whole drink through.

Thanks to Commander Whitehead, Schweppes Tonic is now sold in 50 states of the Union.

So whether you mix yours with gin, or vodka, or rum—or drink it straight, like our friends in the picture—make sure you get the *real stuff*.

The one and only *Schweppes* Tonic. It's curiously refreshing.

inventive pieces of Ogilvy's self-aggrandisement, a feature that appeared on the front of the OB&M in-house magazine. With a picture of himself next to one of Charlemagne to prove the physical likeness, Ogilvy proclaimed he'd finally found proof that "your Chairman" is indeed descended from this greatest of legendary medieval kings.

At the recollection Roman smiles and says, "It was not a joke. It was serious. But we all kind of smiled, 'that's David being David.' He was a man of enormous ego, but he had this self-aware humor. He didn't take himself that seriously. He was an actor. When I started doing the research [for his biography, *The King of Madison Avenue*] I found over and over, the things he said about his life were almost true, but not quite. He embellished."

Perhaps the best line he ever wrote, certainly the one for which he was most known, was for an advertisement that created an eighteen-month waiting list of potential customers: "At 60 miles an hour the loudest noise in this new Rolls-Royce comes from the electric clock."

When it was pointed out that it had an unfortunate precedent, some might say beyond coincidence, in a 1933 Batten, Barton, Durstine and Osborn (BBDO) ad "The only sound one can hear in the new Pierce Arrow is the ticking of the electric clock," his insouciant response was that he didn't steal it from Pierce Arrow, he stole it from a British motoring magazine article. Ogilvy was a fanatically hard worker. "He had no hobbies," says Roman. "He'd take two briefcases home every night. In *Mad Men* you see people leaving the office to go to bars, to go to the theater. David would leave the theater to go back to the office. I think it broke up his second marriage; he said that he was going to travel the world, do all these things but he didn't. He just worked."

He smoked, but a pipe only, and liked a drink—"I find if I drink two or three brandies or a good bottle of claret, I'm far better able to write"—but strongly disapproved of drunkenness. He was discreet in any personal antics, deeply attractive to women as he was.

WITH THE 1963 PUBLICATION of *Confessions of an Advertising Man*, Ogilvy's fame skyrocketed. It's an advertising manual with clearly prescribed chapter subjects but written in a jaunty, informal

The Rolls-Royce Silver Cloud—$13,995

"At 60 miles an hour the loudest noise in this new Rolls-Royce comes from the electric clock"

What __makes__ Rolls-Royce the best car in the world? "There is really no magic about it—it is merely patient attention to detail," says an eminent Rolls-Royce engineer.

1. "At 60 miles an hour the loudest noise comes from the electric clock," reports the Technical Editor of THE MOTOR. Three mufflers tune out sound frequencies — acoustically.

2. Every Rolls-Royce engine is run for seven hours at full throttle before installation, and each car is test-driven for hundreds of miles over varying road surfaces.

3. The Rolls-Royce is designed as an *owner-driven* car. It is eighteen inches shorter than the largest domestic cars.

4. The car has power steering, power brakes and automatic gear-shift. It is very easy to drive and to park. No chauffeur required.

5. The finished car spends a week in the final test-shop, being fine-tuned. Here it is subjected to 98 separate ordeals. For example, the engineers use a *stethoscope* to listen for axle-whine.

6. The Rolls-Royce is guaranteed for three years. With a new network of dealers and parts-depots from Coast to Coast, service is no problem.

7. The Rolls-Royce radiator has never changed, except that when Sir Henry Royce died in 1933 the monogram RR was changed from red to black.

8. The coachwork is given five coats of primer paint, and hand rubbed between each coat, before *nine* coats of finishing paint go on.

9. By moving a switch on the steering column, you can adjust the shock-absorbers to suit road conditions.

10. A picnic table, veneered in French walnut, slides out from under the dash. Two more swing out behind the front seats.

11. You can get such optional extras as an Espresso coffee-making machine, a dictating machine, a bed, hot and cold water for washing, an electric razor or a telephone.

12. There are three separate systems of power brakes, two hydraulic and one mechanical. Damage to one will not affect the others. The Rolls-Royce is a very *safe* car—and also a very *lively* car. It cruises serenely at eighty-five. Top speed is in excess of 100 m.p.h.

13. The Bentley is made by Rolls-Royce. Except for the radiators, they are identical motor cars, manufactured by the same engineers in the same works. People who feel diffident about driving a Rolls-Royce can buy a Bentley.

PRICE. The Rolls-Royce illustrated in this advertisement — f.o.b. principal ports of entry — costs **$13,995.**

If you would like the rewarding experience of driving a Rolls-Royce or Bentley, write or telephone to one of the dealers listed on opposite page. Rolls-Royce Inc., 10 Rockefeller Plaza, New York 20, N. Y. CIrcle 5-1144.

ABOVE *One of the most famous advertising lines of all time; Ogilvy's Rolls-Royce advertisement.*

style, anecdote mixed with homily. Like Reeves' *Reality in Advertising,*
it was intended as little more than a manual for his agency and the
original print run was five thousand copies. Well over a million have since
been sold.

It was a brilliant new business tool, containing chapters guaranteed to
catch the eye of potential clients: How to be a Good Client, How to Build
Great Campaigns, How to Write Potent Copy, How to Make Good
Television Commercials, How to Make Good Campaigns for Food
Products, Tourist Destinations, and Proprietary Medicines—and,
typically mischievous, ending with "Should Advertising be Abolished?"

His efforts had paid off; by now, he was one of the very few advertising
names known outside the business and fifteen years after he had opened
it, his agency was billing $34 million and ranked twenty-eighth in New
York. But although there was a residual reputation for great creative work,
it was still hanging on early campaigns like Hathaway and that single
Rolls-Royce advert. Increasingly, when it came to turning out campaigns,
O&M was being seen as creatively near bankrupt.

Part of the problem was Ogilvy's advertising ideology, which seemed
heavy-handed and inconsistent throughout the fifties and into the sixties.
He was fanatical about detailed analysis of the results of advertising
research—"This is what I learned from Gallup. I'm obsessed with it"—
and about prescribing how an ad should and should not be created. He
developed rules for concepts, copy, and layouts with hard facts about
effectiveness for any given technique, such as: "Five times as many
people read headlines as body copy"; "Research shows that it is dangerous
to use negatives in headlines"; "Readership falls off rapidly up to fifty
words of copy but drops very little between fifty and five hundred words";
"Always use testimonials."

Like Reeves, Ogilvy's proclaimed approach was mechanical—take these
ingredients, mix them my way and *voila*! Guaranteed Advertising Success.

THE REEVES/OGILVY RELATIONSHIP was complex.
Says Roman, "They respected each other, they were rivals. David was his
student when he came here. Rosser was a big deal, a big copywriter. David
adopted him as a mentor. They used to lunch together regularly. Rosser

"The consumer isn't a moron; she is your wife. You insult her intelligence if you assume that a mere slogan and a few vapid adjectives will persuade her to buy anything. She wants all the information you can give her."

DAVID OGILVY

used to say "Do you want to be admired or do you want to be successful?" And he felt there was a dichotomy there. But David brought taste and style . . . so they parted ways on that. They parted ways on a lot of things. When David divorced Rosser's wife's sister, that was a break, on a personal basis. And Rosser really brought up David's son for many years."

There were other personality differences. While Ogilvy was regularly (and rightly) praised by the press for his business ethics and integrity, the Bates agency was in constant trouble with the Federal Trade Commission concerning overclaiming and false and rigged product demonstrations, all driven by Reeves' desire to ram home demonstrable product differences.

Yet Ogilvy never stopped proclaiming his belief in Reeves' advertising philosophy, telling him he was "his most fervent disciple." The whimsy of those early advertisements and the small eccentric clients on which Ogilvy had built his early creative reputation had gone. There was a good reason—he lost money on both Hathaway and Schweppes. The agency was now large and in the major league, winning the vast Shell business in 1960 to go with earlier successes from General Foods and Lever Brothers. These larger clients liked the reassurance of rules and formulae—they found the serendipitous nature of campaigns that work apparently just because the character happens to have a comedy beard, unnerving. "After that," said Ogilvy of the Shell win, "we changed from being a creative boutique, and got to be a proper agency."

Throughout the agency the rules were applied, and they hobbled the output of the creative department, particularly the art directors. This bothered Ogilvy little, as he didn't have much faith in the intuitive nature of his creative staff anyway. Bart Cummings quotes him in *The Benevolent*

Dictators: "Most of the people who do advertising campaigns are rather run-of-the-mill people. If you impose a dogma on them that is research-based, you save them from wasting so much of the clients' money." Cliff Field, an English creative director under Ogilvy, said he "threw up his hands at art directors."

So it's hardly surprising that the ads started to look repetitive—just a glance at page 39 and you can see how similar they were. Looking back in 1982, Ogilvy himself said, "For years it was difficult for us to persuade an art director to work at Ogilvy & Mather." Yet the ads had some quiet elegance and style. As Ogilvy put it, "I have come to believe that it pays to make all your layouts project a feeling of good taste, provided that you do it unobtrusively. An ugly layout suggests an ugly product."

Reeves was ever dismissive of Ogilvy's more refined approach, once describing the sort of ad Ogilvy would do if he had the Anacin account as "Cecil Beaton or Truman Capote reclining on a bed in a Viyella bathrobe with a caption of 'You'll never know you drank that gin if you brush your teeth with Anacin.'"

Cruel—but pointed. And with that parody of Ogilvy's cultivated approach from the man who brought you hammers pounding the inside of your head, you get a perfect illustration of a battle of ideologies that had been running within agencies since the late nineteenth century, almost from the day that copywriters started working.

It was a pendulum swinging between those who believed in the hard sell, like Reeves, and those who believed in a softer sell, like Ogilvy—between an unadorned utilitarian "reason to buy" appeal and a more emotional "image" approach. But while Ogilvy and Reeves were battling it out, the advertising world was beginning to look another way, noticing the pendulum swinging in a new dimension, to an approach that altogether transcended the old extremes.

3 The Unlikely Hero

" I know the copywriters tell the
art directors what to do and
the account executives tell the
copywriters what to do. "

PEGGY OLSEN MAD MEN

Reeves once warned against originality, citing it as "the
most dangerous word of all in advertising," and every day that belief was
enforced throughout Madison Avenue, to the detriment of the work and
dismay of the creative people. Their lives were ever more driven by
research, which in turn reinforced the status quo, since only that which
already exists could be researched. Add to that their servility to clients
who were happy only with the familiar, and it's inevitable that originality
would be stifled.

In most agencies the creative work was merely a functional job. The
power within the organization rested with the account people, those who
fronted the agency and liaised with the client. It was they who brought the
requisition for the campaign to the copywriters, they who frequently
decided the particular strategic platform on which the ads had to be built,
they who judged whether or not they wanted to present it to the client,
and they who eventually did so.

Next came the writers. Received wisdom had it that advertising was
"salesmanship in print" and as salesmanship was spoken sales patter, it
followed that the "word" had primacy over pictures. At the bottom of the
heap were the art directors or visualizers, whose opinion was rarely sought,
who hardly ever received the brief and never met the clients. They did the

writers' bidding, usually simply executing his or her instructions as to how the ad should be laid out and illustrated.

Not even the creative director had much of a say, and few had the autonomy of Don Draper at Sterling Cooper. It was the account men—almost exclusively men—who were the judge and executioner on all creative work, with the power to reject, edit, and even personally rewrite if they so wished. The account executive, like an obsequious waiter groveling to a valued diner in a bad restaurant, took the order to the creative kitchen who served up exactly what the client wanted—usually what he'd had the day before and the day before that. And if the client wanted ketchup on his sea bass, then the waiter saw to it that the kitchen people damn well gave him ketchup on his sea bass.

ALL THIS CHANGED on June 1, 1949, when Bill Bernbach, together with Maxwell Dane and Ned Doyle, opened Doyle Dane Bernbach (DDB). To decide the running order for their names in the agency title, they'd tossed a coin. They also agreed on doing away with the commas that usually ran between proprietary names: "Nothing will come between us, not even punctuation," said Bernbach. The agency was twelve people in all and they started what would remain one of the two biggest upheavals in advertising until the growth of the Internet—the upheaval now known as the Creative Revolution.

Bill Bernbach's philosophy was so radical it was almost incomprehensible: "We have no formula at all. The only common denominator in our ads is that each one has a fresh idea. We present the story in a fresh and original way." Agency writers, and particularly art directors, constrained in the executional straitjacket of a Reeves or Ogilvy dogma, found it astonishingly liberating.

For Bernbach it had been a comparatively short haul in advertising from fledgling copywriter to agency owner. Born in 1911, one of four children to Russian and Austrian Jewish middle-class parents, and brought up in the Bronx in an unremarkable childhood, he went on to study music, philosophy, and business administration at NYU. It was as good a mix as any for a future in advertising, although at the time that was far from his intention.

He left college in Depression-shrouded 1932 and he took a job his father had arranged for him in the mail room of a local brewery, Schenley Distillers. While he was there, he took to creating ads for Schenley's American Cream Whiskey, almost little more than doodling, and sent them off to the company's agency, Lord & Thomas. A few months later he was amazed to see one of his ads in a paper.

"I had gotten to know [Schenley President] Rosenstiel's secretary . . . and she took me under her wing, and a very powerful wing it was too," he recalled in Bart Cummings' *The Benevolent Dictators*. She encouraged him to establish credit for the ad by visiting L&T to see if he could look through their files to find a copy of the letter he'd enclosed with his suggested ad, proving it was his idea.

"I was reading a book of poetry at the time, Kahlil Gibran, a romantic Indian poet that I, at that moment, was in love with. And I went to call on this girl who was in charge of the files up at Lord & Thomas and she said, 'What are you reading?' I showed it to her and, lo and behold, she was a devotee of Kahlil Gibran. So she went to the files and sure enough, there was the letter." The upshot was a job in the marketing department at Schenley, and Bernbach's career in advertising was launched.

MAJOR EVENTS WERE also developing in his personal life, described by Doris Willens in *Nobody's Perfect*:

"The Twenty-first Amendment to the Constitution had been ratified on December 5th, 1933, repealing Prohibition. Ex bootleggers turned into distillers. At the young Schenley company, headquartered in an elegant midtown brownstone, Bill wrapped bundles of 'The Merry Mixer,' a promotional brochure of cocktail recipes much in demand across wet again America. A young Hunter College graduate, Evelyn Carbone, addressed the labels, often glancing up to see if Bill, as he often did, re-buried his head in a book. She loved his passion for books, seeing him as a kindred spirit in a coven of bootleg-era survivors."

Fairly soon they were seeing each other regularly and the increasing warmth of his welcome in the Carbone family was in inverse proportion to the freeze he experienced in his own home. His mother could not reconcile herself to the idea of her children "marrying out" and was implacable in

ABOVE *Bill Bernbach in his office in 1966*
with several famous DDB campaigns shown
behind him.

her hostility to the relationship. Increasingly, Bernbach was swapping a Jewish life in the Bronx for an Italian one in Brooklyn, and in 1938 he made the break final by eloping and marrying Evelyn before a justice of the peace.

Meanwhile, his career had been given a massive leg-up by the larger-than-life figure of Grover Whalen, an alleged PR and marketing expert, who had been New York City's police chief during Prohibition and who had subsequently joined Schenley as Chairman of the Board. In 1935 he was put in charge of organizing the New York World Fair that was to open in 1939, and he took the young Bill Bernbach with him to work in his offices in the Empire State Building and at the site in Flushing Meadows. In May 1939, *Time* reported, "the fair as it stands today—a $157,000,000 extroversion of Mr Whalen's fantastic extrovert personality—gives him fair claim to the title of the greatest salesman alive today."

The proximity to such a central character in New York business life, together with the experience gained in dealing with the corporate sponsors, press, and politicians, was a fast track for the young Bernbach fresh out of a small company marketing department. And as his primary function was in creating publicity—he claimed to have written speeches for Whalen and "many prominent people"—his grounding in commercial communications continued on a broader scale.

But when the fair wound up in 1940 Bernbach had to start all over again. Now with a taste for advertising—he said, "I thought it might be a good idea to ghost for some products instead of people"—he looked for a job as a copywriter. Evelyn was still working for Schenley's, and through her Bernbach was introduced to William Weintraub, the owner of the agency that handled Schenley's advertising.

Up against two qualified rival candidates and with no actual advertising work to show, Weintraub asked Bernbach to write him a letter justifying why he should be chosen. The letter did the trick.

BY HAPPY ACCIDENT Bernbach was assigned to work with Paul Rand, one of the greatest figures in US commercial art and on his way to becoming a godfather of American graphic design. Rand believed that design should have "the utmost simplicity and restraint," and he applied his modernist, European philosophy across his body of work for book publishing, advertising, and branding, including logos as familiar and famed as IBM, ABC, UPS, and Enron.

It was the next great influence on Bernbach's career, not just Rand hinself but the fact that they worked together. At Weintraub, the separation between copywriter and art director was not as rigidly applied as elsewhere. The two men, just three years apart in age, were free to create in tandem, working on ads from the start of the assignment with no primacy of writer over art director. Their collaboration developed over free-flowing conversations that included lunches and roaming round galleries, all informing and illuminating Bernbach's development as a communicator.

To Bernbach, this fusion of writer and art director became so natural as to be unquestionably the only way for creative people to work and for advertising ideas to be developed. It was the only way of producing complete ideas that are born from thinking of the way that words can most effectively combine with, and compliment, pictures.

His stay at Weintraub and his relationship with Rand was upended in 1941 by Pearl Harbor. Bernbach spent just two months in the army, a pulse rate of up to 148, making him unfit for duty. He came back to New York and after a short stint as Director of Post-war Planning at Coty Inc, the cosmetics marketer, rejoined advertising at Grey. Like Weintraub, Grey was a "Seventh Avenue" agency, a predominantly Jewish firm. The sobriquet derived from so much of the garment business—traditionally the client base of Jewish agencies—being located on Seventh Avenue.

By 1945 he was copy chief, familiar to clients and agency management alike and clearly hitting his stride. But he didn't like the way things were run at Grey, a regimented, unprogressive place with little imagination or room for creativity. And within two years he'd written his famous letter.

But at Grey, his letter and his views were ignored; the agency's Board was happy with the way things were, and didn't want his troubling new ideas on management structures and company philosophy.

Amongst the Grey client roster was a budget department store that sold mainly women's apparel and accessories. This was Ohrbach's—"A business in millions, a profit in pennies"—and Bernbach had worked on the account personally, again in direct collaboration with an art director he'd hired, Bob Gage. Their work had caught the eye of Nathan Ohrbach, the owner, and he urged Bernbach to leave and set up his own business with the store as his first client. Initially Bernbach demurred, but when a few months later Ohrbach came back and said he was pulling the business out of Grey anyway, Bernbach took the plunge and started his own agency.

NED DOYLE, then a Grey account director, was at face value a curious choice of partner. He was ten years older than Bernbach, a fighting Irish ex-marine, physically imposing, with an active service record in the Pacific and almost a parody of the type; hard smoking, hard drinking, and hard swearing. Bernbach was soft spoken, quietly mannered, five foot seven, nonsmoking, abstemious with alcohol, unremarkable to look at.

When he first met Bernbach, Doyle described him as a "nice little guy, very creative with gold-rimmed glasses, and on the scared side." But then, perhaps most people he met for the first time appeared to be a little on the scared side—they probably were. This is Doyle several years later on the phone to the DDB Los Angeles office chief, giving him advice on handling his client Ernest Gallo who was making trouble: "You go to a store and buy a power mower. Put it in your car and drive to the winery. When you get there, shove it up his ass and turn on the power."

Even Roger Sterling would have been impressed.

That Bernbach could ever conceive such an idea, let alone speak it out loud, was quite unthinkable. Yet the two hit it off to such a degree that they were happy to risk it all and hang up their shingle together. To Bernbach's start up philosophy can be added Doyle's; as Doris Willens writes, he wanted to create an agency "whose principles we could believe in. . . . To give [the client] the work we think he should have, provided it fit his goal. . . . Not to wonder what the client's wife is going to say about the advertising."

No ketchup with their sea bass then.

Doyle had a friend, Maxwell "Mac" Dane, who already ran a small agency at 350 Madison Avenue with walk up offices—the elevator stopped at the floor below and you had to climb the stairs to the remaining floor. So with premises, a few staff, lines of credit, a little seed money from the partners (Bernbach put in $1,200), and a generous goodwill advance on fees from Nathaniel Ohrbach, the business was off and running.

" I have no rules for people. I just want them to do what comes naturally to them, but to do it in an effective way. So that they're doing their own thing, but they're doing it in a sharp and disciplined way to make it work."

BILL BERNBACH

Bernbach took two key creative people: Bob Gage as head art director, and Phyllis Robinson as copy chief, the only writer. "A copy chief of me," as she later said. Gage and Robinson endorsed Bernbach's philosophy. As Gage later said in *DDB News*, "The combination of the visual and the words, coming together and forming a third bigger thing, is really fundamental." Robinson added, "The whole being greater than the sum of its parts—this was something very new. It seems astonishing to think about it now because it seems like the most natural thing in the world."

PHYLLIS ROBINSON was born in 1921 and brought up in New York. Attracted to advertising as a child, she even told her high school teacher that that was the world she wanted to work in, a wildly eccentric notion for a young girl at that time. She remembers being fascinated by ads, taking particular delight in the Burma Shave billboards along the highways. Each told a sequential part of a story in verse and as you sped by, the tale unfolded, billboard by billboard.

But in her late teens, she had "developed a little political and social awareness—things were falling apart in Europe and I had the feeling I should do something a little more serious," so she chose to study sociology at Barnard College in Manhattan. She graduated in 1942 and, true to her ideals, started in public housing. But the war was to change everything.

"My husband was drafted, pulled out of Harvard, and I tried to get public housing jobs, or something related to it, as I followed him around on his southern tour. But I couldn't so I just got work wherever I could. At that point I was beginning to get back to the idea of some kind of writing, advertising, or promotion."

Robinson's first agency copywriting job was with a Boston agency, Bresnick & Solomon, while her husband, a future psychologist, was back at college. Then they moved to New York and she started at Grey, writing fashion promotions, where she caught Bernbach's eye: "I worked directly under him and he did a lot . . . to tighten up my writing and make it more vivid." Eventually, he thought enough of her, early as it was in her career, to ask her to join him in his new venture. She didn't need to think twice.

As lucky breaks go, they don't come much more propitious. There was no way for her to know it at the time—this was, after all, just another risky little breakaway with no reason to imagine the success to come—but that one conversation was to propel Robinson into the very highest plane of New York advertising history.

Although her decisions were usually subject to Bernbach's ultimate sanction, she had enormous influence over the conduct and development of the agency's creative output. It was she who for the next decade or so approved work and employed writers, combing their books for indications that here was a talent that would fit with DDB's strange new attitudes. Don't forget, there was little training ground for DDB—no college or rival agency was turning out writers practiced in its way of thinking and working. It was too new. Any writer hopeful of getting work there had to be either studying their methods and attempting to reproduce them in their own time, or osmotically producing work in DDB's style for their current agency, almost inevitably doomed to be rejected by their own management but hopefully appreciated in an interview with Mrs. Robinson.

In those early years she hired more women than men, observing with either undue modesty or remarkable candor that it was perhaps because she felt easier being a boss to women. Judy Protas was her first hiring, from the advertising department of Macy's. Paula Green was hired with a background of writing for magazines and agencies, including work in account service. Lore Parker, an Englishwoman born in Germany with no copywriting experience, got her job purely on the strength of a letter she sent in to DDB. Later she would say, "The most successful headline I ever wrote was 'Dear Mrs. Robinson.'"

Protas, describing the office in her very first days at the agency says, "We were squeezed into the penthouse and Ned Doyle looked at me and said, 'Kid, can you work hanging from the chandeliers?'"

ABOVE *Phyllis Robinson; DDB's first copy chief.*

BOB GAGE, Robinson's opposite number as head art director, had been hired a few years earlier by Bernbach at Grey. He was yet another hopeful who had nervously removed pieces of work from his folio the night before his interview. Gage was worried that Bernbach would not be impressed merely because they'd been published, and replaced them with speculative work of his own. The meeting went well, discussing their own views of advertising and finding much common ground—"I had at last found someone who not just tolerated new ideas but demanded them"—and he was hired. Gage, too, had been influenced by the spare style of Paul Rand and an even bigger influence was Alex Brodovitch, art director of the radical *Harper's Bazaar* magazine.

Brodovitch's was an extraordinary story; a Russian émigré who had lived the prototypical bohemian life in pre-war Montparnasse where he had immersed himself in just about every possible artistic movement in the dizzyingly evolving scene around him. That hectic artistic development was manifest in his obsession with never doing the same thing twice, an utter abhorrence of the unoriginal. Art Kane, for a time the unparalleled fashion and music artist photographer, said, "He taught me to be intolerant of mediocrity. He taught me to worship the unknown." Hiro, the fashion photographer, echoed, "I learned from him that if, when you look in your camera, you see an image you have ever seen before, don't click the shutter."

Gage, too, carried into DDB this almost neurotic desire to be fresh every time, exactly in accord with what Bernbach wanted. But he had two more qualities to add to the mix that marked out his work. One was extreme self-effacement; when asked to supply a biography for an award from the New York Art Directors' Club many years later, he wrote merely: "Bob Gage, Vice President and Head Art Director of Doyle Dane Bernbach since the day it opened its doors." In a business noted for noisy egos and monstrous self-satisfaction, this was almost bashful; such quiet modesty meant he was incapable of producing the loud, chest-beating advertising work of a Rosser Reeves.

Gage's other quality was that he was simply a thoroughly good man. In a particularly crucial quote, from the Art Directors Hall of Fame, about the criteria for employment at DDB, a quote that tells us not just about

Gage, but also about Bernbach and the whole ethos of the agency, Bernbach said, "You have to be nice and you have to be talented. If you're nice, but untalented, we don't need you. If you're talented, but a bastard, we don't need you. No one exemplifies the nice and the talented better than Bob Gage."

As Gage said, the agency's creative solutions were derived directly from cold facts about the product itself. But that was just the start. His achievement, initially with Robinson and Bernbach and then with a succession of later DDB writers, was in warming and molding those "cold facts" into a body of work of genuine warmth and emotion. The simple humane charm in the stream of work moved reader after reader, viewer after viewer with an emotional impact transcending anything necessary for the purely utilitarian purpose of advertising.

The sheer vivacity and freshness in the work they started to produce reflected the childlike euphoria in the first few years of the agency. Phyllis Robinson later said, "We all had, including Bill, the feeling that we were let out of school—you know, no more teachers, no more books . . . a tremendous feeling of freedom, just for starters."

Behind every famous campaign there's usually an open-minded client, deserving recognition at least for judgment, taste, and, quite often, bravery. The easy, comfortable solution is to do what you've done before, what everyone else is doing; the farsighted client knows this is the worst solution. Nathan Ohrbach was one such client.

Encouraging and applauding his advertising teams to come up with fresh and original thinking, it showed in his choice of agency; he'd employed Weintraub in the mid forties, then moved the account to Grey when Bernbach started doing interesting work there. Finally, like a commercial Medici, he encouraged and backed the breakaway. It paid off. His business grew, enabling expansion into suburban New York, Newark, Los Angeles, and elsewhere.

OHRBACH'S ADVERTISING already had some fame around town as one of the more noticeable and radical pieces of retail work, and this was boosted early in the agency's life by the ad that one could argue marked the start of the Creative Revolution. To today's

ABOVE AND OPPOSITE *Ohrbach's advertising created by DDB in the late 1950s.*

I found out
about Joan

The way she talks, you'd think she was in Who's Who. Well! I found out what's what with *her*. Her husband own a bank? Sweetie, not even a bank *account*. Why that palace of theirs has wall-to-wall *mortgages!* And that car? Darling, that's horsepower, *not* earning power. They won it in a fifty-cent raffle! Can you imagine? And those clothes! Of course she *does* dress divinely. But really...a mink stole, and Paris suits, and all those dresses...on *his* income? Well darling, I found out about that too. I just happened to be going her way and *I saw Joan come out of Ohrbach's!*

Ohrbach's

© 1958 by Ohrbach's Inc.

34TH ST. OPP. EMPIRE STATE BLDG. · **NEWARK** MARKET & HALSEY · "A BUSINESS IN MILLIONS, A PROFIT IN PENNIES"™

sensibilities it may seem patronizing and condescending, but those were different times and it gained attention through its very playfulness.

A man is carrying a grinning woman under his arm, flat like a cardboard cutout, with the headline "Liberal Trade-in. Bring in your wife and just a few dollars . . . and we'll give you a new woman."

The idea was Bernbach's—described by Gage as "the most visual copywriter I ever worked with"—but the copy was left to Phyllis Robinson to write. (Bill was now mostly concerned with ideas and headlines, others could do the "wiggly bits," the actual body copy.)

The message of the ad is loud and clear: new fashionable clothes, a complete makeover at bargain prices. But the novelty was in the way it was said, a key DDB attribute, playing with the *notion* of advertising by borrowing language from elsewhere—auto sales for example—and applying it here to your wife. Intriguing and entertaining the reader, but all the while selling.

In the same year, 1952, the headline "If you are over or under 35 . . . you need SNIAGRAB (spell it backwards)" over a picture of a white-coated man pointing straight at you, spoofed another style of advertising, this time pharmaceutical. But the idea was not so much satirizing other ads as having fun with the whole notion of buying and selling and advertising, a conspiratorial wink between seller and buyer.

A few years later, in 1959, they produced another startling ad, in which a cat wearing a fashionable hat and smoking a cigarette in a cigarette holder makes catty remarks about a friend behind her back, revealing that she isn't as wealthy as she seems—she achieves the illusion by, shocking to reveal, shopping at Ohrbach's!

Ohrbach's was like a client magnet for DDB. Other New York businesses looking for an agency would ask around to find who did the advertising and then approach DDB to handle their account. In fact, in the following decade DDB rarely, if ever, made a formal new business presentation, as often as not being approached by clients rather than the other way round.

ONE INTERESTED ENQUIRY came from Whitey Rubin, put in charge of a small Jewish bakery in Brooklyn by its bank in a last-ditch attempt to turn the business around and keep it from bankruptcy.

For thirty years they had traded successfully selling bagels, onion rolls, and challahs to an almost exclusively Jewish clientele. The problem arose when the company extended its range to a variety of breads baked to appeal to a wider market. The Jews didn't like it and the gentiles didn't know about it. Quoted in Robert Glatzer's *The New Advertising*, on his first sampling of the new breads Bernbach said, "Mr Rubin, no Jew would eat your bread. If you want more business, we have to advertise to the *goyim* [non-Jews]."

So the initial original thought by DDB for Levy's was a media idea, concentrating exclusively on a specific market. Next, they contradicted the received wisdom that good bread must be soft, and they began to promote the nourishing values of Levy's Oven Krust White Bread with a series of intelligently but simply-argued ads. One asked "Are you buying a bread or a bed?" and another, against a drawing of a fat child contrasting with an athletic child, "Is his bread a filler-upper or a builder-upper?" This was good hard-working stuff, and a slow improvement in sales followed.

Then Phyllis Robinson wrote a radio campaign around a small boy whose mother continually tried to correct his faulty pronunciation of "Wevy's Cimmimum Waisin Bwead." His pay-off line, "I wuv Wevy's," became a catchphrase, boosting Levy's name recognition and fame. But the taste of things to come was an ambitious claim, with a simple layout graphically illustrating the thought: over three pictures of the same piece of rye bread, quickly disappearing as bites are taken out of it, were the words "New York . . . is eating . . . it up!"

New York certainly started nibbling. It was advertised as "Levy's real Jewish Rye," itself a little contrived as there's nothing particularly Jewish about rye bread. And Rubin, anxious about anti-Semitism, couldn't initially understand why its Jewish provenance needed to be flagged up at all. "For God's sake," countered Bernbach, "your name is Levy's. They're not going to mistake you for a High Episcopalian."

In the increasingly worldly and sophisticated market that New York had become, maybe that touch of exoticism was exactly what the brand needed. What came next, created by writer Judy Protas and Bill Taubin, generally reckoned to be one of the very best of DDB's earlier art directors, reinforced and amplified that exoticism. In one large picture and one simple line they linked one minority—the Jews—to all the other emerging minorities making their presence felt.

Subway passengers became aware of posters with large, engaging pictures of the people you'd least expect chewing through a hunk of Levy's. And if they looked authentic, that's because they were authentic. Howard Zieff, the photographer, who went on to direct some of the very best commercials of the sixties before starting a new career as a Hollywood director recalls, "We wanted normal-looking people, not blonde, perfectly proportioned models. I saw the Indian on the street; he was an engineer for the New York Central. The Chinese guy worked in a restaurant near my midtown Manhattan office. And the kid we found in Harlem. They all had great faces, interesting faces, expressive faces."

It would be easy now to dismiss the whole campaign as stereotypical, even condescending, but not then—far from it. These ads were startling for the simple reason that such people weren't usually seen starring in advertising. New Yorkers reveled in it, demanding copies of the Levy's posters as well as the bread. It reflected and celebrated their contemporary multi-culturalism, and for the immigrants it helped "normalize" their status simply by making them seem an accepted, normal part of society.

It is a wonderfully simple idea, little more than the strategy, photographed. Yet within it you can find all the unique hallmarks of a DDB campaign: wit, surprise, freshness, fun, simplicity, directness, a credible promise—and again that knowing but friendly nod and wink toward the consumer.

THIS, IN ESSENCE, was what was so different about DDB. The new graphics, the design, the choice of typefaces, the style of copy— all are fascinating in their own right, but in the end they're not the answer, just part of the means to the end. What these ads were doing was signaling a changed relationship between those who would sell and those who would buy. A relationship based not just on respect for the people's taste but for their intelligence and ability to discern what really mattered in their lives from the purely transitory.

To a client, his product is life and death, something that if only the wilful public would try, they'd realize would change the course of their lives; but

ABOVE *1964–65, DDB's "You don't have to be Jewish . . ."*
campaign for Levy's, a huge commercial and cultural success.

to a busy housewife or commuter, it's often no more than an irksome purchase on the way to something else. DDB had the honesty to recognize this, and the candor and skill to communicate that recognition, making the potential buyer an ally rather than a target. "The artist rules the audience by turning them into accomplices," as Arthur Koestler put it.

Bill Bernbach's people, without impudence but based on self-respect and a belief in their ability to communicate properly with the public, ended the slavish deference toward the client and the product. Bernbach recalled a conversation with a new business prospect: "'What would you say, Bill, if you were told exactly where to put the logo and what size it would be [on the advertisement]?' I had $10 million riding on my answer and I said, 'I would say we're the wrong agency for you.'"

It wasn't a question of either Reeves' hard sell or Ogilvy's respectful but rule-based formulaic sell. It took the best of both and shucked off the remains. As Bob Gage had observed, no DDB ad would ever be created without a rigid consumer proposition at its center, the philosophy at the heart of Reeves' USP idea. And no DDB ad would ever be created without deep respect, not just for the consumer's intelligence, but also the consumer's true priorities. Bill Bernbach stopped selling dreams and started selling the truth—wrapped in wit.

4 Lighting the Touchpaper

"Have we ever hired any Jews?"
"Not on my watch . . . we've got an Italian."

ROGER STERLING AND DON DRAPER **MAD MEN**

The clients, big and small, national and local, flocked in. All were taken on DDB's terms, which included a tacit ethical standard; the product must be honest and worthy of the money that the agency would be asking the public to pay for it.

Jim Raniere, an art director who joined DDB in 1961, contrasts the ethos at DDB with agencies that friends had joined: "Never lie, never never say anything about a product that it can't do."

The account for *The Book of Knowledge*, a children's encyclopedia, came and then went when a new copywriter found it was too complicated for his eight-year-old daughter. On those grounds he refused to work on it. The rumpus was elevated to Bernbach who took the book home with him. The next morning he pronounced that the product was flawed and the client was told the agency no longer wanted to advertise it.

High-minded, yes. It wasn't just posturing, it was in reaction to the generally bad name that advertising had around town. And it was driven by the new breed of people that Bernbach and his managers were employing, people of a completely different stock with a completely different mindset.

Up until the late 1950s, advertising had been seen by account people mainly as an alternative to Wall Street, with good salaries at a fairly early age and a respectable life dealing with upper levels of client companies in an influential milieu. Copywriters, too, tended to be from comfortably educated backgrounds. You might get the odd Italian as a visualizer but who cared? The client never knew who he was, let alone got to meet him. In the late 1950s, Jerry Della Femina, a young copywriter, was told in an interview at JWT that on the basis of his name alone, Ford Trucks "wouldn't want your kind on their account."

But beneath the well-shined Oxfords of the comfortable WASP account executives patrolling the Madison Avenue sidewalks, the world was turning and several elements were beginning to coincide to make the Creative Revolution almost inevitable.

AS ITALIAN-AMERICANS like Della Femina were demonstrating, there was a growing confidence among the second and third generation ethnics, people born from the mid–1930s onward. Their Ellis Island parents and grandparents, perhaps cowed from the oppressive experiences in the Europe from which they had escaped, were desperate to conform, to assimilate, and become American. Deference was their watchword, but as familiarity and security came, so too did self-assurance, and this new generation no longer "knew their place."

Very few had any reservations about applying for white collar jobs in advertising agencies, an aspiration that probably would never have occurred to their parents. Although there were the occasional setbacks, increasingly foreign names were appearing on doors along the agency corridors, and ethnic origins were a matter of pride.

George Lois remembers his interview with Lou Dorfsman at CBS Radio in the fifties; Dorfsman, son of Polish Jews, rolled George's name around his mouth and said, "Lois, Lois—is that a Jewish name?"

"I'm not a fucking Jew," countered Lois, "I'm a fucking Greek!"

A key Bernbach remark, "You always have to work in the idiom of the times in which you live," could be applied to the people most appropriate to produce that advertising. This group of creative people had none of the cultural inheritance of the older guard, the pre-war New York. And they certainly didn't respect the creative legacy of the existing inhabitants of the agencies; quite the reverse. They felt alienated and appalled by it, responsible as it was for so much of the general antipathy toward advertising. It was neither their language nor their imagery. And one word above all others crops up over and over again, with deep disdain, in the contemporary interviews and records of their views.

Phony.

It was the one thing they did not want to be, and the one thing they resented above all others about the current advertising. Commercials with actors playing reassuring doctors; perfectly coiffed housewives trilling about the perfection of their cake mix; and men in white lab coats holding up test tubes and booming in authoritative voices some drivel about "ingredient X."

IT WASN'T JUST THEIR ORIGINS, it was also their youth. America had just invented the teenager, had begun to give these youths presence and influence, and they were the first to benefit. Rebellion was in the air, with the icons of James Dean and Marlon Brando to emulate. There was even, for the more anguished, Holden Caulfield, J.D. Salinger's young, disaffected hero from *Catcher in the Rye*.

"We came home full of kick-ass energy and the GI Bill to educate us. Tradition, school ties, and old boys clubs became relics," said Jim Durfee, a war veteran. At the time, he was a copywriter at JWT in Detroit, but later he was to co-found Carl Ally Inc, one of the very best agencies of the decade. That energy found a period of literally fantastic artistic expansion and experimentation to feed and fuel it. As George Lois wrote in a 2010 *Playboy* article, "It was an inspiring time to be an art director like me with a rage to communicate, to blaze trails, to create icon rather than con. The times they were a-changin."

From the white-tie audiences at Carnegie Hall to the marijuana-clouded coffee shops of the beat poets on Bleeker Street, the black beebop jazz clubs of Harlem to the cooperative galleries of Tenth Street, nothing stood still.

With Manhattan's frenetic building and rebuilding program, the world's leading architects added their prestigious signatures to the cityscape. In 1959, Frank Lloyd Wright's futuristic Guggenheim Museum was finished one year after Mies van de Rohe's beautiful Seagram Building, fifty-two sheer stories sheathed in bronze and bronzed glass, the classic functionalist skyscraper. In furniture, European influences from the Bauhaus onward removed the stuffing and streamlined the design—by the 1960s no agency with any self-respect could have anything other than Charles Eames chairs in their reception area.

The spread of the 35mm camera, with its changeable lenses and greater portability brought magazines an indispensability and urgency as exciting news vehicles. Until television usurped it in the late 1950s, *Life* magazine had its purple period, sponsoring not just dramatic photography but superb illustration; its lofty literary content included the first publication of Hemingway's *The Old Man and the Sea*.

IN MUSIC, ART, AND LITERATURE a dazzling explosion of imagination and energy fired a million incandescent ideas across the decade, some false and quickly sputtering, others arcing with a brilliance into the next century. But it was ignited against a social background that was far from settled.

Jazz writer Jeff Fitzgerald describes jazz in the 1950s as taking on "a restlessness, reflecting an undercurrent of trepidation lying just beneath the surface. Jazz became more cerebral, more introspective . . . the music of a generation in transition, searching for its identity in a world populated by increasingly invisible, intangible perils. In a world living under the shadow of the atomic bomb and the creeping menace of Communism and an increasingly automated society feeling the control of its own daily existence slipping away with the push of every button, it is perfectly logical that the music should reflect that nameless angst."

He could have added the tension caused by the rapidly growing awareness of racial injustice, and it was the black population that was the driving force behind jazz. Musicians like Art Blakey, Charles Mingus, and Thelonious Monk took the music into infinitely more complex forms. Free jazz "experiments" were taking place at the Five Spot on Cooper Square, organized by musicians like Ornette Colman.

More accessible were the Modern Jazz Quartet, Dave Brubeck, and Lester Young. But perhaps the best evocation of the jazz of the era, hypnotizing the hip crowd at Birdland and the Village Vanguard, was the poignant foggy moan from the trumpet of Miles Davis, the man Kenneth Tynan called "a musical lonely hearts club."

It could hardly have been in greater contrast to that other massive trend in music; in 1954 Bill Haley and the Comets released "Rock Around the Clock" and the dance hall, the record player, and the juke box would never be the same again.

The visual and performing arts were even more explosive. Jackson Pollock, Willem de Kooning, and friends in the New York School threw paint around in an excitable way never seen before, creating the genre known as action painting. Meanwhile, for a very different audience, Mark Rothko was commissioned to paint a set of murals for the opulent new Four Seasons restaurant.

Between Tenth and Twelfth Street, in reaction to the stultifying and exclusive establishments of Fifty-seventh Street and Madison Avenue, artist-owned galleries gave an outlet to every experimental idea. Artists like Jim Dine and Claes Oldenburg were collaborating with poets and musicians such as John Cale in the phenomena of the Happening, a partially free-form, audience-participation performance art (which gave rise to a misplaced lingerie ad of the time, a woman floating in space with the headline "I dreamt I was at a Happening in my Maidenform bra").

And in the mid 1950s an art director at Benton & Bowles asked the name of the hopeful blonde female illustrator who'd just shown her folio to a colleague in the office next to his. "That wasn't a chick," he laughed, "I've got his name somewhere . . . er . . . Andy Warhol."

In the Village book shops and coffeehouses, jazz/poetry fusions were achingly hip. Jack Kerouac appeared with a jazz group at the Village Vanguard on Seventh Avenue in 1958 and recorded readings of his prose and poetry with the saxophonists Al Cohn and Zoot Sims. Free-form impromptu poetry readings—one notably earnest performance was a reading of the Manhattan telephone directory—were a regular, if often meretricious, stimulus for impressionable young minds.

From the early 1950s, Washington Square had been the focus for the emerging folk scene, with groups and individual folk singers gathering for impromptu open-air sessions. Thriving, it spread to specific clubs and by January 24, 1961, fresh from the Midwest, the nineteen-year-old Bob Dylan knew enough to head for the Café Wha? at 115 MacDougall Street.

ABOVE *A party at Andy Warhol's studio, The Factory
(231 East 47th Street), New York, August 1965.*

He blew in, snow on his coat, and asked to perform a few Woody Guthrie songs. It was his first appearance in the city.

At the Gaslight Club, a "basket house" (so-named because the artists' remuneration was the cash in the basket passed round amongst the patrons), Allen Ginsberg recited "Howl," his terrifyingly powerful evisceration of everything he felt America had become. Earlier, in the same club, Jack Kerouac had read from *On the Road*.

Cinemas were showing *Rebel Without a Cause* and *On the Waterfront*, dramatizing youthful angst and alienation, while *The Seventh Seal* and *Seven Samurai* intrigued audiences with a growing appetite for foreign directors with a completely different feel for film. At the theatre, Tennessee Williams' *Cat on a Hot Tin Roof*, Eugene O'Neill's *Long Day's Journey into Night*, and Arthur Miller's *Death of a Salesman* all penetrated themes embedded deep within society—and all won Pulitzer Prizes.

As for literature, you took your pick from books, essays or poems from William Faulkner, Henry Miller, Ayn Rand, Tennessee Williams, Truman Capote, James Baldwin, Richard Yates, John Cheever, Isaac Asimov, Saul Bellow, Ernest Hemingway, Norman Mailer, Philip Roth, John Updike . . . the list goes on.

This was the background to the formative years of this new generation of creative people. Whether they immersed themselves in all, part or none of it is not really the point; the fact is that this was their seedbed, seeping osmotically into all creative endeavor. It couldn't help but inform and illuminate their work.

BY 1960, JWT had doubled their 1950 billing to $250 million, retaining the number one spot. Their growth neatly reflected the decade's overall doubling of national advertising spend, up from $5.7 billion to $11.96 billion, evidence of the boom in business accelerated by the growth of TV advertising. But DDB had spectacularly outstripped the market with a hundredfold increase, taking them from $500,000 in 1949 to $46.3 million ten years later. A creditable client list of all product types and sizes (although they still lacked a major packaged goods client), from Coffee of Colombia to Rheingold Breweries, Philip Morris Alpine Cigarettes to Max Factor, Chemstrand to Clairol, defined an agency that was now firmly grounded. And a succession of campaigns began to demand that their competitors take them seriously.

For Polaroid, the first camera to produce a print within sixty seconds of the picture being taken, DDB produced several campaigns, each as radical as any advertising the public had ever seen. The previous agency, BBDO had completely missed the point and produced messy, uninspiring work based on a mishmash of propositions, including price, which served only to make the product look like a cheap gimmick.

On taking over the account in 1954, DDB zeroed in on the product benefit with a "live" TV campaign that appeared on Steve Allen's *The Tonight Show*. During the transmission Allen would take a picture on stage, maybe walking into the stalls to snap a member of the audience, and then talk about the camera while the picture developed. Showing the print to the audience was like the climax and reveal of a conjuring trick, always eliciting applause. How simple, direct, and desirable, to have an unsolicited live TV audience applaud your product on national TV.

Then, in 1957, Polaroid introduced a highly sensitive black–and–white film, and again dramatic simplicity did the trick. The art director, Helmut Krone, hired fashion photographer Bert Stern to take tight close-up pictures of characterful faces, some known and some anonymous. In full-page ads, these dominated the page: every pore, every line, every shadow clear and faithful. Simple copy by Bill Casey told you all you needed to know with the minimum of fuss. There's seldom been a better example of letting a good product sell itself.

ANOTHER TREND in DDB's work started to become noticeable. In contrast to the rigid laws on the use of space laid down by Ogilvy, DDB art directors were quite prepared to play with the imagery, with the page itself, to make the point visually. If advertising had always been regarded as sales talk in print, DDB was frequently doing demonstration in print.

To dramatize Flexalum dirt-resistant window blinds, Bernbach suggested a picture of a tennis ball bouncing off the slats. In another campaign, Helmut Krone showed a photo of a gift-wrapped package in a thin vertical space up the side of a page of *Life* magazine. When the reader

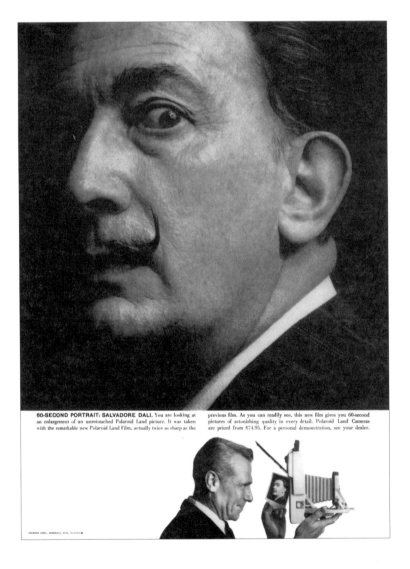

60-SECOND PORTRAIT: SALVADORE DALI. You are looking at an enlargement of an unretouched Polaroid Land picture. It was taken with the remarkable new Polaroid Land Film, actually twice as sharp as the previous film. As you can readily see, this new film gives you 60-second pictures of astonishing quality in every detail. Polaroid Land Cameras are priced from $74.95. For a personal demonstration, see your dealer.

ABOVE AND OPPOSITE *1958 DDB ads for Polaroid, featuring Salvador Dalí and Louis Armstrong. Instant picture, instant success.*

FIRST SHOWING OF A NEW POLAROID LAND FILM. This is an enlargement of an actual 60-second picture of Louis Armstrong. It was taken with a new film, just introduced, which is twice as sharp as the previous film.

With this latest development, the Polaroid Land Camera not only gives you pictures in 60 seconds, but pictures of exceptional clarity and brilliance. Polaroid Land Cameras start at $72.75. The new film can be identified by a star on the box.

held the page up to the light, as invited "for an X-ray peek at a great gift," they saw a bottle of Ancient Age ("If you can find a better bourbon, buy it"), apparently on the inside. It was illustrated on the reverse side of the page and showed through in the light.

You got the point at one glance in one of DDB's greatest-ever ads, opposite, when Bill Taubin tore a strip off a picture of the sea to advertise a new faster service from New York to Tel Aviv for El Al Airlines. The way the ad worked on the eye was the demonstration itself. El Al's budget was relatively small, a fraction of that of even most domestic airlines and DDB could have imitated the approach of all other carriers, using little more than flight schedules printed on the page, with no attempt at any personality. But with El Al, they went further than just new visual ideas—there was a new verbal excursion as well.

El Al was one of Bernbach's many Jewish accounts. While it wasn't remarkable that they should have so many, what was remarkable was the way they handled their Jewishness. Far from hiding it, as Whitey Rubin of Levy's had been inclined to do, DDB celebrated it, and wrote their ads in Borscht Belt idiom. A full page advertisement with a picture of Noah's Ark made the point: "We've been in the travel business a long time," a terrific example of how words can take off from the picture to make a further point.

While the Italians were infiltrating the art department, it's difficult to overemphasize the role the Jewish writer and Jewish idiom played in the Creative Revolution. If you look at the roster of the artists, architects, designers, musicians, and particularly writers who were illuminating the fifties, you'll see an extraordinary percentage of Jews. It had its effect; the Yiddish vernacular and Jewish humor were creeping into the New Yorkers' daily language. Few advertising agencies, dominated as they were by pallid WASP values or an incipient Anglophilia, had seemed to notice it, but as DDB's doors were open to the immigrant and the Jew, the people who lived and breathed these things, it was only natural that it would end up in their work.

SO ON THE VERY VERGE of the 1960s, from many and varied directions, apparently unrelated circumstances converge. We can connect them. In the world's greatest modern city, a massive economic

expansion creates a huge need for the raw product of the advertising business, the ads themselves. The audience for this outburst is a demographically younger, newly wealthy, and curious American, on the edge of a consumer boom—and thoroughly tired of the advertising it's been fed. A brand new medium is sweeping the country and revolutionizing advertising practice, bringing with it opportunity and the chance to experiment.

The doors of a few agencies are being opened to a completely new breed of creative person, one who sees no value in looking back, and who demands to do things in a radically new way. The images and references that will influence their work crackle around in their heads, fizzing from one of the greatest cultural eruptions the world has seen.

In one agency, DDB, those same people are given greater autonomy and prestige, and a new way of working together, which not only overturns the nature of their output but doubles their influence within the business. This financially successful, creatively led agency is no unproven flash in the pan; for ten years now it has been proving that research does not know everything and, as Bernbach recognized publicly, cannot be used to come up with ideas. That, as his agency had slowly been proving, was the job of these new creative people.

As these circumstances converged, intertwined, coalesced, and re-formed, it was time for those creative people to take control.

5 Thinking Small

"They did one last year, the same kind of smirk. Remember, *Think Small*. It was a half-page ad on a full-page buy. You could barely see the product."

HARRY CRANE **MAD MEN**

T he most famous part of the most famous campaign was born out of accident and confusion. At least half of the creative team who conceived it had doubts—and if it hadn't been for the intervention of the client, one of the greatest ads ever written would never have been created.

The task was utterly daunting; to sell a small, basic, ugly, economical, foreign car to a market enthralled with huge, chrome-finned, gadget-stuffed, home-built gas guzzlers. Initially, a number of the people who worked on the Volkswagen (VW) account had misgivings. With the revelations of the full horrors of the Holocaust little more than a decade old, Bernbach, although clearly not bothered himself, had to make considerable effort to persuade his agency to take the account in the first place. As George Lois said, "We have to sell a Nazi car in a Jewish town." Lois' parents had emigrated to the US from central Greece before the war, and he was implacable in his opposition; tales of Axis behavior in Greece hadn't endeared him to any idea of cooperation.

Additionally, the business was at DDB only as a sprat to catch a mackerel; one of Bernbach's attempts at talking Lois around was to tell him, "We'll take it for just a year and use it to get GM." It's probable he meant it too; it seems a perfectly reasonable business decision, if a little cynical. And it worked later in a different category—their much lauded campaign for El Al netted American Airlines in 1962.

Lois remained unpersuaded, but international events took a hand. He was sitting in his office one day: "It had those fogged glass windows and I could see Bill lurking outside. Then he opened the door a crack and stuck his head round the corner, like in *The Shining*—'Heeeere's Johnny!'—and said, 'Look at this'. Then he shoved a newspaper through the gap and held it up so I could read the headline; 'Germany sells fighter jets to Israel'. He said 'It's alright, see?' So eventually I agreed."

Discontent rumbled on though. Lois remembers one prank when he made a small "flip" book with a VW logo on the bottom of the first right-hand page. As you flipped the pages, the legs and arms of the VW symbol quickly and neatly rearranged themselves—into a swastika.

He was showing it to a bunch of creative people when Bernbach walked by. "Hey Bill, Bill, hey, come here, have a look at this."

Bernbach watched the little dance of digits, expressionless.

"Very funny George—now burn it."

Lois went to work on the station wagon, the even less glamorous variant and only alternative to the basic "saloon." "Basic" is the operative word for the then very alien VW.

THE BEETLE—although not referred to as such by VW until the late sixties—already had a toehold in the United States, thanks to US servicemen returning from Europe. It was originally designed by Ferdinand Porsche as the KdFWagen (*Kraft durch Freude Wagen*, literally "Strength through Joy Car") in 1933, under the patronage of no less than Adolf Hitler. By September 1939 mass production had still not started, and then with the outbreak of hostilities across Europe, the VW Wolfsburg factory was converted to wartime vehicle production. It wasn't until the war was over that the first models started to leave the plant, when the factory was restored to car manufacture under the management of two British army officers, Colonel Charles Radclyffe and Major Ivan Hirst, producing cars for the transportation of the occupying forces.

As a concept, it was a good one. The objective was a car designed to be uncomplicated, reliable, and inexpensive. It was to be within the reach of every German family, to enjoy the new freedom of the burgeoning *autobahns* of the 1930s. The engine was air-cooled, as simple as a contemporary motorcycle engine. Mounting it in the back avoided the need for a transmission and the hump of a transmission tunnel on the floor between the rear seats, which made the car even simpler. It also created more room inside a comparatively small cabin. The floor pan, chassis, and suspension were equally uncomplicated.

It was this idea—a cheap utilitarian European car conceived for the 1930s working man and then built to carry servicemen around a war-blitzed country—that had to be sold to a nation used to soft suspension, plush upholstery, and powerful engines. Glamorous it wasn't. The potential for its success can be gauged from the reaction of Ford Motors, after it was offered the VW factory for free: "What we're being offered here isn't worth a damn!" Or British car executives, who could also have had the plant and designs for nothing: "The vehicle does not meet the fundamental technical requirement of a motorcar . . . it is quite unattractive to the average buyer."

DDB had won the account from JM Mathes in 1958. VW's modest sales throughout the fifties were perhaps partly still generated by word of mouth, by the personnel returning from Germany, where the United States Army remained a visible presence. And there was a nascent market for smaller, imported European cars; there were a few enlightened motorists who were beginning to see through the smoke and mirrors of Detroit's annual model changes and built-in style obsolescence. In response, in 1959, Ford, Chrysler, and GM all decided to produce their own "compacts." This burgeoning change in attitude, and the fact that most European cars performed poorly on America's highways and freeways, built as they were for smaller roads and shorter distances, meant that VW's market was now coming under threat.

So that year, Carl Hahn, who was in charge of VW in the United States, started to look for an advertising agency. He and Arthur Stanton, the New York area VW dealer, trawled up and down Madison Avenue, going to all the big agencies currently without a car account. Though the business was comparatively small, there was plenty of eager attention from the competing agencies.

Hahn hated the presentations, uniformly. Today he says, "It was the only disappointment I had about Americans . . . going up and down

Madison Avenue. The content of the proposed ads was always the same, a beautiful house, very happy people in front, beautifully dressed—and a glamorous car. Even that in most cases was not photographed but illustrated . . . with a stupid caption. But [they] didn't have [any] life. I had more and more presentations. I was desperate, I told Arthur this is just impossible, we need an agency that fits our product."

It's unclear why DDB were not on Stanton's original pitch list as he was a fan of Ohrbach's advertising and was already using the agency for his dealership advertisements. But eventually he suggested a visit and Hahn agreed. He gives a fascinating insight into the difference between the conventional agency presentations of the time and the infinitely more laid back and candid DDB approach. Other agencies, and some clients, regarded DDB's refusal to prepare speculative work for a pitch as arrogant; DDB insisted it was honest. Until you really got to work on a client's business, how could you possibly know enough to do the right work?

"I went to these primitive offices, no big conference room or hall, no ten vice presidents in blue suits with neckties and white shirts, and executive vice presidents and senior vice presidents; there was just a man sitting on his desk in a windowless room, called Bill Bernbach by name, and he showed me work he'd done for El Al and more. . . . I decided what to do: offered for the first six months an advertising budget of half a million or so, which he accepted."

BERNBACH CHOSE HELMUT KRONE as art director and Julian Koenig as writer. Krone was a second generation German American who had once briefly owned a VW. Born in 1925, he is now enormously respected as one of the most influential art directors in US history, even though for thirty years—almost his entire working life—he worked only at DDB. He was fastidious and exacting in his work; he went to Germany several times to extract as much information as he could about the car. He believed that design in the service of a product should be indivisible from that product; the look and feel of the page, the attitude and body language of the artwork should reflect the attitude and body language of the product.

He also believed that including logos in ads was unimportant, a turn-off in fact, because as soon as a logo hits the retina it signals "advertisement" and thus becomes an invitation to turn the page. But that doesn't mean he was undisciplined or careless with his clients' problems; because of his belief in the indivisibility of "look" and "message" he would create for any client on whose account he worked a page layout that was instantly recognizable from twenty paces as uniquely theirs—even without their logo. It would also be a look that was universally applicable and workable; VW ads today, fifty years and literally millions of worldwide executions later, are still a recognizable reflection of his original template.

The layout for the VW campaign wasn't particularly original, but it does perfectly exemplify Krone's philosophy. In using a squared-up halftone photograph, a centered headline, and three columns of type, he was only sequestering what was then sarcastically known at DDB as the "Old JWT No. 1" or "The Ogilvy Layout," referring to a lazily used hand-me-down layout found at agencies that were seen by DDB as creatively inferior. But the fact that it was well worn didn't deter Krone; the car was simple and uncluttered, and its pitch to the customer was direct and honest. Look at the ads on the following pages, right down to the choice of typeface—how else to describe their appearance other than uncluttered and honest?

WHERE KRONE DEPARTED dramatically from the JWT/Ogilvy template was by taking this stripped down approach through to the photography. It was unheard of back then for almost any product, let alone a car, to appear naked of props, be they crunchy gravel settings in front of Connecticut country houses or doormen at plush Upper East Side apartments helping elegant women laden down with hat boxes. But the VW image was direct simplicity—so the ads also had to look simple and direct.

Krone was quiet, methodical, and unemotional. Some people found him difficult and moody. In Jack Dillon's novel *The Advertising Man*, written while Dillon was still working at DDB as a copywriter, he describes the first morning for his central character, copywriter Jim Bower. He's at his new "hot" agency, working with Brook Parker, the fictional Head of

ABOVE *Helmut Krone; "a brooding kind of genius."*

Art. After enduring a tense silence that goes on for nearly an hour while Parker sits stock-still, Bower tentatively suggests an idea for the ad they're supposed to be working on. For several seconds there's absolutely no reaction from Parker. Then, without shifting his gaze, he speaks: "We don't do ads like that here."

Very Helmut Krone. As was Krone's taciturn response to the novel, even though he hadn't been positively identified: "I would never have called myself Brook Parker." Krone had a fanatical attention to detail and shared Gage's obsession with doing the original. Carl Fischer, a photographer Krone liked to work with, remembers a particular Polaroid shoot:

"On the first day the ad had to have ten children in it and we had carefully worked out all the ideas for the ten children. So we're out on a beach somewhere near LA with a whole bunch of account people, a bunch of copy people, a bunch of clients . . . and ten children and ten mothers (and ten teachers which is required in California) and the food people in these catering trucks—it was a major operation. And we all knew what we were supposed to do . . . but Helmut decided it's okay—but it should be better! So we stopped the shoot and sat down on the beach talking about how it could be better, as if all these people weren't standing around waiting. Really it was a disaster but finally we came up with something and the client was happy. But the point is that Helmut suffered through everything he did. It had to be better, it had to be perfect, it had to be original, it had to be done the way nobody had ever done it before and that's hard to do."

Fischer liked him: "A lot of people said he was cold and remote and difficult to work with. I found him very easy . . . we got along very well." Ted Shaine, a DDB art director describes him as "a brooding kind of genius, not very personable." People put his remoteness down to a very tough childhood, apparently with a furiously strict father and, as he told Fischer, a mother who was a Nazi sympathizer.

"But he did have a sense of humor," Fischer says, "it's just it needed to be discovered. I first met him at a cocktail party. In those days I had a trapdoor above my studio and I used to take a lot of pictures from high up, looking down either at 45 degrees or straight down. And Helmut and I were introduced and he looked me up and down and said, 'I expected you to be a lot taller.'"

JULIAN KOENIG, the writer, was the maverick type that often attracted Bernbach. Of comfortable birth into a family of lawyers, he nevertheless lived the life of the Bohemian nonconformist, at one time being part owner of a semiprofessional baseball team who played at a field in suburban Yonkers.

"This is just as TV was coming in to cover baseball and just as the color-line was fading in baseball because Jackie Robinson became the first black ball player back then—so we had a dream enterprise. It was semi-pro. We played good teams, a lot of whose players went to the majors. We had a big turnout on our first night, around six thousand people, but the city was viciously corrupt . . . never fulfilled their part of the bargain, which was to install toilet facilities. So you have the visions of women going under bushes and lifting their dresses. And once they do that they are never going to return."

He became a copywriter in 1946 "for lack of anything else. I had written half a novel . . . which I sent to the Little Brown company, which was the firm that Norman Mailer had succeeded with. He had tried twenty-nine publishers, the thirtieth was Little Brown and they accepted *The Naked and the Dead*, so I figured I would skip the twenty-nine and go straight to Mailer's publisher, and I was rejected. I became a copywriter out of lack of any other opportunity. I'd been at law school prior to all that and I wasn't going back."

Koenig's first agency was tiny, with small accounts. "I was a junior copywriter or an apprentice copywriter. My office was in the file room . . . and you learn that if you can work there, you can work anywhere. It was good discipline. I was hired for $20.50 a week, which was less than the $25 I had been promised. So we organized the agency's union, which I ended up leading. Then I left."

By 1950 he was working and doing well at a bigger agency, Hirshon Garfield, but, in typical beatnik fashion, he suddenly gave it all up and traveled to Europe with his wife. It was an interesting time for a Jew to be in Germany. He remembers being at the beer festival in Munich, asking directions, and recalls with irony, "Nobody had ever heard of Dachau, which was ten minutes outside the city."

They stayed for six months "until our money ran out . . . then I returned to Hirshon Garfield and was made copy chief and given a 50 percent increase in salary." However, he had had very little work published so he took a leave of absence to work on a book. The "book" wasn't of the literary type, it was for gambling on the horses. "I perfected my betting abilities. So I supported my wife and two children betting on the races. I had a horror of becoming the world's oldest working copywriter. I could have continued at the track because I would have made more money than I would have working in advertising—but I got offered a job at the one agency I wanted to work at, which was Doyle Dane Bernbach."

Koenig's main claim to fame until then as a writer was a much-applauded campaign for Timex watches: "Takes a licking and keeps on ticking." Amongst other "torture tests," a Timex watch was immersed in the Dead Sea, put through a washing machine's spin cycle, and even hosted by the digestive tract of a family pet. But this wasn't the campaign that got him into DDB. He'd had a tip from Rita Seldon, a DDB writer he'd worked with previously, about a job going there. Bernbach looked through his book and, in the now regular pattern, hired him on the strength of an ad for a root beer that had been rejected by a previous client.

CARL HAHN HAD ALREADY written the VW strategy. It was the measure against which all the agencies he had visited had failed. He wanted everything about VW to be honest, transparent, and straightforward—the product, the pricing, the dealers, even down to the policy of changing the external appearance of the car as little as possible. This was in direct contrast with Detroit who deliberately made major design changes every year to make their cars obsolete and force an image-conscious public to continue forking out for the latest models.

It was therefore a simple matter for Ed Russell, the head account man, to write a strategy calling for honest advertising. The first line of the "Statement" as the strategy paper at DDB was called, was "The VW is an honest car." Reading the body copy you immediately appreciate the candor with which Koenig approached the reader, very much following the strategy. In one way it's Page One advertising copy, packed with product features and USPs. But it reads like a friendly chat—enthusiastic, yes, but more of a tip from one friend to another about something he or she ought to know.

"We just took [the] product and said what made it good. And we were fortunate that there was a lot to say about the VW."

JULIAN KOENIG

What is more startling is the apparent challenge in the headlines, not just of the reader but of the product itself. They were all fundamentally negative, and that simply wasn't done.

It's impossible to imagine the jaw-dropping amazement with which Detroit executives and their advertising agencies must have viewed these ads from a rival car manufacturer, apparently advising their potential market that the car was a failure and of limited ambition. But it was all part of the same candor—tell 'em like it is and it'll intrigue them and then amuse them. But don't leave it there—while they're busy appreciating you, gently insinuate some sales points.

THERE'S A CURIOUS STORY around the origination of the "Think Small" ad, one which enhances the already noble role of another bold and prescient client who would put his money behind such an unorthodox and, at that point, unproven and manifestly risky strategy.

The ad was originally meant to be a corporate ad, advertising the marque rather than a specific model, and it showed three huge American cars. Koenig wrote the headline "Think Small" to contrast with this visual. Then, as Koenig remembers it, "Helmut wouldn't use it. And he who controls the [layout] pad in those days, controls the ad. So we finally come up with Willkommen, which I didn't want but Helmut wanted, and with 'Think Small' in the copy. In DDB, copywriters and art directors didn't go to the client with ads, the account people went. So they presented the ad, came back and said 'Willkommen is out'. Fortuitously, Helmut Schmidt— the client—didn't want Willkommen, which I knew they wouldn't because that made it a German car, and we wanted to be as American as apple strudel, as the ad says. He saw the line 'Think Small' and thought that should be the ad."

Think small.

Our little car isn't so much of a novelty any more.

A couple of dozen college kids don't try to squeeze inside it.

The guy at the gas station doesn't ask where the gas goes.

Nobody even stares at our shape.

In fact, some people who drive our little flivver don't even think 32 miles to the gallon is going any great guns.

Or using five pints of oil instead of five quarts.

Or never needing anti-freeze.

Or racking up 40,000 miles on a set of tires.

That's because once you get used to some of our economies, you don't even think about them any more.

Except when you squeeze into a small parking spot. Or renew your small insurance. Or pay a small repair bill. Or trade in your old VW for a new one.

Think it over.

ABOVE AND OPPOSITE *1959–60, early examples from the DDB campaign for VW.*

Ugly is only skin-deep.

It may not be much to look at. But beneath that humble exterior beats an air-cooled engine. It won't boil over and ruin your piston rings. It won't freeze over and ruin your life. It's in the back of the car for better traction in snow and sand. And it will give you about 29 miles to a gallon of gas.

After a while you get to like so much about the VW, you even get to like what it looks like.

You find that there's enough legroom for almost anybody's legs. Enough headroom for almost anybody's head. With a hat on it. Snug-fitting bucket seats. Doors that close so well you can hardly close them. (They're so airtight, it's better to open the window a crack first.)

Those plain, unglamorous wheels are each suspended independently. So when a bump makes one wheel bounce, the bounce doesn't make the other wheel bump. It's things like that that you pay the $1585* for, when you buy a VW. The ugliness doesn't add a thing to the cost of the car. That's the beauty of it.

©Volkswagen of America, Inc. *Suggested Retail Price, East Coast P.O.E., Local Taxes and Other Dealer Delivery Charges, if Any, Additional.

How much longer can we hand you this line?

Forever, we hope.

Because we don't ever intend to change the Volkswagen's shape.

We play by our own set of rules.

The only reason we change the VW is to make it work even better.

The money we don't spend on outside changes we do spend inside the car.

This system gives us an immense advantage: Time.

We have time to improve parts and still keep most of them interchangeable.

(Which is why it's so easy to get VW parts, and why VW mechanics don't wake up screaming.)

We have time to put an immense amount of hand work into each VW, and to tough each one like a $6,000 machine.

And this system has also kept the price almost the same over the years.

Some cars keep changing and stay the same.

Volkswagens stay the same and keep changing.

No point showing the '62 Volkswagen. It still looks the same.

No heads will turn when you drive a '62 Volkswagen home.

(Maybe an eagle-eyed neighbor will notice that we've made the tail lights a little bigger. But that's the only clue.)

Everything else on the outside is right where we left it in '61.

Inside is another story.

We've put all our time and effort into improvements that matter.

The '62 VW runs more quietly. There are new clutch and brake cables (as well as new steering parts) that never need maintenance. Heater outlets front and rear for more even heating. Easier braking.

One change is literally a gasser. We've added a gas gauge. Our first.

A few die-hards may think we've stolen some of the VW's sporting flavor. But the gas gauge may be more useful than you'd imagine. It will not only tell you whether your tank is E or F; it will prove you're driving a '62.

It could make 1962 go down in VW history as the year of the big change.

Lemon.

This Volkswagen missed the boat.

The chrome strip on the glove compartment is blemished and must be replaced. Chances are you wouldn't have noticed it; Inspector Kurt Kroner did.

There are 3,389 men at our Wolfsburg factory with only one job: to inspect Volkswagens at each stage of production. (3000 Volkswagens are produced daily; there are more inspectors

than cars.)

Every shock absorber is tested (spot checking won't do), every windshield is scanned. VWs have been rejected for surface scratches barely visible to the eye.

Final inspection is really something! VW inspectors run each car off the line onto the Funktionsprüfstand (car test stand), tote up 189 check points, gun ahead to the automatic

brake stand, and say "no" to one VW out of fifty.

This preoccupation with detail means the VW lasts longer and requires less maintenance, by and large, than other cars. It also means a used VW depreciates less than any other car.

We pluck the lemons; you get the plums.

So one of the most famous advertising headlines of all time was, if not exactly written by a client, certainly spotted and promoted by one. Koenig says, "I'm told in Germany they credit the ads to the copywriters Helmut Schmidt and Julian Koenig."

According to Koenig, it took the famously grumpy Krone two days to bring himself to put the line down on paper. Meanwhile, the requirement had changed from a corporate to a product ad so it needed to show a VW. Initially, this further exasperated Krone by suggesting that logically, this meant the car should be shown small, which he didn't want to do.

But he calmed down and, encouraged by Bob Gage and others around him, worked fastidiously at the layout. Eventually he placed a small car at a slight angle in the top left hand corner of the page—and an advertising icon was created.

THE CREDIT FOR "LEMON," too, has a convoluted path. "The art directors used to put their advertising ideas up on the walls," says Koenig, "and Helmut had put up my headline 'This VW missed the boat'. Rita Seldon came into Helmut's office and she said, 'Lemon!' Helmut said go tell Julian and she walked about thirty-five feet down to my office and said 'Saw your ad, Lemon!' I said, 'Terrific'. So Lemon became the ad and I took my headline and made it into the first line of copy."

This version is disputed by George Lois, who claims that Koenig wouldn't listen to Seldon, and it took her two weeks to persuade him to make the change. But as the two have been, and still are, in a high-energy spat over who did what on all sorts of ads they worked on, some of which were created fifty years ago (with one of them even going to the extent of preparing an ad for *The New York Times* to "set the record straight") it's difficult to know who to believe. But it is to Koenig's credit that he'll cheerfully admit that the provenance of the world's two most famous advertising headlines were not his and his alone.

The impact of the campaign was immediate, with the ads getting unusually high readership figures. Imported car sales at that time had halved in two years under the onslaught of the simultaneous launch of brand new compacts from all the major players in Detroit. But in the same period, VW sales actually rose by nearly 25 percent.

Reinforced by this obvious endorsement from the only meaningful measure, the marketplace, DDB forged ahead with the campaign in the style which Bernbach, Krone, and Koenig had set. In less than a year, Koenig had left to set up his own agency with George Lois, their big fallout yet to come. But there were plenty of other brilliant writers to carry on the idea, amongst them Bob Levenson, who went on to write the definitive book about the agency's groundbreaking creative output, *Bill Bernbach's Book*. Other art directors, too, would come along to work on the account, but all followed the template and attitude set by the original team.

In TV, too, executions were conducted with the same spare directness, but still with the knowing wit of "Think Small" and "Lemon." In one, "Funeral," the solemn occupants of a long funeral cortege of huge cars are shown one by one as the voice of the deceased intones over each:

"I, Maxwell E Snavely, being of sound mind and body, do hereby bequeath the following: To my wife Rose, who spent money like there was no tomorrow, I leave $100—and a calendar. To my sons Rodney and Victor, who spent every dime I ever gave them on fancy cars and fast women . . . I leave $50—in dimes. To my business partner Jules, whose only motto was 'spend, spend, spend', I leave nothing, nothing, nothing. And to my other friends and relatives who also never learned the value of a dollar—I leave a dollar." At the end of the procession we see a young man driving a VW Beetle, clearly upset. "And finally, to my nephew Harold, who oft times said 'a penny saved is a penny earned' and who also oft times said 'Gee Uncle Max, it sure pays to own a Volkswagen', I leave my entire fortune of one hundred billion dollars."

In another, "Snow Plow," one of the consistently most admired TV ads of all time, principally for its simplicity, we see a car covered in snow traveling through heavy drifts to a shed where the driver gets out and opens the shed doors. We hear the roar of a powerful engine and he drives out on a snow plow. The voice-over says just twenty-seven words: "Have you ever wondered how the man who drives the snow plow—drives to the snow plow? This one drives a Volkswagen—so you can stop wondering."

Ad after ad after ad, the same playful self-deprecating wit, the same chatty, knowing but economical copy—and always the same instantly recognizable layout and look. Very few people ever appeared in the ads,

Think It over, New York, Chicago, San Francisco.

33 years later, he got the bug.

How to make a '54 look like a '64.

You do yours.

ABOVE AND OPPOSITE *Further DDB ads for VW, from 1963–80. VW advertising is still with DDB today.*

Can you still get prime quality for $1.26 a pound?

A pound of Volkswagen isn't cheap compared to other cars. But what you pay for is the quality. Prime quality.

Just look at what you get for your money:

13 pounds of paint, some of it in places you can't even see. (So you can leave a Volkswagen out overnight and it won't spoil.)

A watertight, airtight, sealed steel bottom that protects against rocks,

rain, rust and rot.

Over 1,000 inspections per one Beetle.

1,014 inspectors who are so finicky that they reject parts you could easily ride around with and not even detect there was anything wrong.

Electronic Diagnosis that tells you what's right and wrong with important parts of your car.

A 1600 cc aluminum-magnesium engine that gets 25° miles to a gallon

of regular gasoline.

Volkswagen's traditionally high resale value.

Over 22,000 changes and improvements on a car that was well built to begin with.

What with all the care we take in building every single Volkswagen, we'd like to call it a filet mignon of a car. Only one problem. It's too tough.

Few things in life work as well as a Volkswagen.

That's about the size of it.

That special paint job is to make it perfectly clear that our Station Wagon is only 9 inches longer than our Sedan.

Yet it carries almost a ton of anything you like. (About twice as much as you can get into wagons that are 4 feet longer.) Or eight solid citizens, with luggage. Or countless kids, with kid stuff.

The things you never think about are worth thinking about, too.

You never worry about freezing or boiling; the rear engine is air-cooled.

You can expect about 24 miles per gallon and about 30,000 miles on your tires.

And you can forget about going out of style next year; next year's model will

look the same.

The most expensive VW Station Wagon costs $2,685: it comes in red and white or grey and white or green and white.

And you won't ever have to go around painting sedans on it to show how small it is. Just park.

The Super Beetle.

The Turbo. Drivers wanted:

there were almost never any props that weren't directly part of the car and very rarely was it shown against anything other than a white background.

THE CAMPAIGN'S IMPACT goes way beyond just VW, DDB, and the New York advertising scene of the early sixties. This campaign, more than any individual ads or campaigns that had gone before, epitomizes the Creative Revolution, and that revolution changed the face of advertising. Ohrbach's, Levy's, El Al were all terrific pieces of work, but none of them was a nationally-advertised brand competing in a mainstream product category.

Of course there had been people creating entertaining, witty, simple, and sympathetic advertising before, people who recognized a value in directness and candor. But they tended to be in isolated pockets and their efforts were easily snuffed out. They were shouted down by the orthodox who believed that empathy had no place in advertising; that anything other than the tried and tested was too risky; that any money spent on making friends with your potential customer was money wasted; that simple repetition, like the pounding of a jackhammer, was the most effective way to get a message to stick; that he who shouts loudest gets heard clearest; that more is more.

These people will forever be confounded and bewildered by the early VW ads, wondering how those who did them ever had the nerve. The consistency of approach and the high standard of thinking has ensured that to this day, when many DDB agencies around the world still handle the VW account, generations of creative people who have followed the original team more than half a century ago feel obliged to try to live up to their standard. Today's VW advertising is still consistently winning awards and selling VW's across the globe.

6 The Word Spreads

"You want some respect?
Go out and get it yourself."

DON DRAPER TO PEGGY OLSEN **MAD MEN**

K rone, still dubious about the campaign said later, "I finished up three ads, went on vacation to St. Thomas, depressed, came back two weeks later, and I was a star."

Mad Men's Don Draper completely missed the point of the "Lemon" ad; "I don't know what I hate about it most," he said. But everyone was talking about the campaign and it wasn't just people in advertising. College students had the ads posted on walls and curious customers were strolling into VW dealerships quoting the copy.

The irony of the VW campaign launching just one year after Detroit's most catastrophic marketing failure, the launch of the Ford Edsel, shouldn't be missed. The two case histories, one for a grotesquely overblown and glitzy automobile launched with unprecedented levels of Madison Avenue flatulence, the other for an honest and functional car announced with self-deprecating but intelligent wit, illustrated perfectly the gulf between DDB and the rest of the business.

One aspect of the Edsel disaster was not lost on Bob Gage. As he half-mischievously put it, "There is a great danger in research as a basis to work from. One of the biggest flops of the century was the . . . what was the name of that car? I don't even recall it now . . . which was an entirely researched design. It had everything everybody wanted, except that nobody wanted it."

This was heady renegade stuff. This was an agency with a major success on its hands desecrating the altar at which Madison Avenue worshipped, laughing at research. The effect on the rest of the business, particularly the new young creative people, was explosive. At last they had a champion that proved that agencies didn't have to be run (and ads didn't have to be done) in the old tired way, and that a creatively oriented agency could credibly be held up as not just a creative but a business success.

There were other small pockets of creative endeavor around New York. CBS under Bill Golden at TV and Lou Dorfsman at Radio had acted as a sort of graphics finishing school, with a stream of future first-class designers and art directors passing through in the mid to late 1950s. Herb Lubalin, a lifelong friend of Dorfsman, who gained notoriety in 1963 as the designer of the eventually banned avant-garde erotic magazine *Eros*, was creative director at Sudler & Hennesey. A noted experimenter with type, Lubalin, like Golden and Dorfsman, attracted a greater share of future creative award winners than this small, mainly pharmaceutical agency should logically have had. Bob Kuperman, later to head the VW group at DDB, Carl Fischer, one of New York's leading advertising photographers for four decades, and George Lois were just three of them.

But none of them had the critical mass and national fame of DDB— John Kennedy, anticipating his 1964 presidential campaign, was said to have asked his staff about "the VW agency." And critically, in the eyes of the young iconoclastic creative people pushing their way upwards, it was recognized to be "Bernbach's place," an agency led by a copywriter, as opposed to an account man.

Jack Dillon explains the implications of this when describing life at DDB as a writer later in the sixties: "There are a lot of writers and art directors in other agencies who, I'm sure, are very creative and able. But they are not working for agencies run by a writer or an art director. They are working for agencies run by businessmen."

Referencing the early days of advertising agencies, he continues, "Writing ads was offered as an extra service by a businessman, not as the main thing that an agency did . . . its status had already been established. Creative people were and are usually under non-creative people. Bill Bernbach changed this. Bernbach was a copywriter and . . . he knew what good and bad advertising were."

Many times since, creative leadership has proved to be less than dazzling. But Bernbach, with Mac Dane and Ned Doyle, was building a glittering business, both financially and creatively. And the thinking amongst the new creative community was if he can do it, so can I.

One person who had already tried was Fred Papert. He had written his first copy in the 1940s for Woolf Brothers men's clothing store in Kansas City while working there as a salesman to pay his way through a journalism course at the University of Missouri.

He had a series of jobs as a "ragamuffin copywriter" at Benton & Bowles and Y&R, and then became creative director at Kenyon and Eckhart. He was fired from that company while working on the Pepsi account, for which he had wanted to do experimental photography at the agency's expense. Joan Crawford, the wife of the Pepsi president, vetoed his request. Papert objected, and summoned by his boss told him no matter who they were, clients shouldn't tell the agency what to do with its own money. His boss said, "You're right. You're also fired."

At his next agency, Sudler & Hennessey, he met and briefly worked with the young George Lois, but he had already started to formulate the idea of having his own place. The lineup for his new outfit was a little eccentric; the four partners were two married couples, Fred and Diane Papert, both writers, Bill Free, an art director, and his wife Marcella, another writer. Sadly it didn't last; within a year Papert was on the phone to George Lois at DDB, offering him his name over the door if he would take Free's place.

LOIS WAS, AND STILL IS, a hugely energetic man, with so much going on in his head he often struggles to get it all out. He talks fast, in a thick Bronx accent, with frequent expletives emphasizing his absolute views. Things—any things—are either sensational or a piece of shit, an idea will either knock you off your ass or it's the worst thing you've ever seen. The phrase George Lois is least likely ever to use? "It'll do."

He was born in 1931 and brought up in an almost exclusively Irish area of the Bronx. "The discrimination against my family from another immigrant population, the Irish, sure didn't bother me, I literally had twenty-five to thirty fist fights with kids in my neighborhood. I won all of my fights, then wound up being friends with everybody.

ABOVE *George Lois. One way or another, he'll knock you off your ass.*

"I went to the greatest high school in the world, a place called Music & Art in New York. It was the greatest institution of learning since Alexander sat at the feet of Aristotle. I got this incredible education, it was kind of a Bauhaus education, 1945 to 1949. And I then didn't know quite what to do, but I figured I better go to another art school because I was aged seventeen and a half and I didn't know where to get a job because it wasn't a field where people were looking for talent. I mean, there weren't many places you wanted to work at—you'd love to work for Paul Rand. You could try to do record album covers or book jackets, etc. So I went to Pratt Institute, paid for by tips I got delivering flowers for my father since I was a kid, because he expected me to be a florist."

From Pratt he was taken on by Reba Sochis as the first employee in her rapidly expanding studio. "In just one day working for Reba, you could learn more than in four years at Pratt or Cooper Union. She was the toughest boss in the world, but she was also the sweetest woman you could hope to know." She was one of the biggest influences on his life, a genuine pioneer; while female copywriters were comparatively plentiful, female designers were almost unheard of, let alone one running her own studio.

After military service in Korea, Lois returned to New York, first to CBS, briefly to Lennen and Newell, where he overturned the agency chief's desk because he'd been rude about his work and then to Sudler & Hennessy, where David Herzbrun first met him: "George Lois was a tall Greek kid with a big nose and a big lopsided grin. He looked as if he'd been nailed together from scrap building materials." He described "the loose limbed way he walked and the way he talked with his hands, his shoulders hunched over."

Herzbrun may be being a little harsh; a contemporary picture reveals strong-jawed matinee idol looks, and in Lois's own words, "I was far better looking than Don Draper." He and Herzbrun were teamed together, while Fred Papert, who was metamorphosing into an account man, was busy trying to get business for the agency. But it wasn't easy, as Herzbrun recalls:

"George had a way of making clients nervous. If they appeared to have any doubts about our work, he could be counted on to say something like 'You fuckin' crazy? This is the best fuckin' campaign you saw in your fuckin' life.' This speech was usually delivered in a tone of mixed fury and contempt while George loomed over the clients with fists clenched." His street-fighting days were certainly not finished; it's possible they're still not over, as he claims to have been in a fight during a recent basketball game in which he was playing—at the age of seventy-nine.

BY 1959, Lois had already done noticeable enough work to breeze into a job at DDB, leaving Papert and Herzbrun behind. His first year was sensational; by his own admission he managed to upset just about everyone at DDB, from Phyllis Robinson and Helmut Krone down, and win more major awards than anyone else. It's possible the two were connected; his lips are never far from his own trumpet and no set of rules was ever going to constrain George.

It may seem counterintuitive to find that within an organization as radical as DDB there were already rigid mores and inflexible cultural tics. But you'll frequently find that creative people within advertising agencies are amongst the most conservative—and tribal—on earth, and they don't like their boat being rocked.

George's first mistake was to spend the weekend before he joined painting his office and moving in his own furniture. Cutting edge though their advertising may have been, DDB's offices were grey and almost dowdy, and George's brilliant white walls and Eames chair stood out as a belligerent style challenge from the new boy. Then his energy, bellicosity, and irrepressible confidence irritated enough people that eventually a deposition of creatives went to see Bernbach to complain about him. Bernbach listened to them and said (and bear in mind this is George's story), "You don't understand—George Lois is a combination of Bob Gage and Paul Rand." Could there be higher praise?

Robinson had already called Lois in to admonish him for rudeness to Judy Protas over an idea he'd had for the news broadcasts for CBS television: "I broke it down into twenty-four small space ads all throughout the newspaper that said 1 PM, 2 PM, 3 PM and each ad was an ad that said every hour on the hour, so when you looked through the paper you saw twenty-four ads, dominating the paper. It was a sensationally brilliant way to do something . . . and the writer comes in . . . and she says, 'No, no, no, no George, you don't understand, we at Doyle Dane don't do small space ads, we only do big ads', at which point I said 'Get the fuck out of my room.' In fact I told four or five writers to get the fuck out of my room. Until Phyllis Robinson called me in and tried to chew me out. We wound up being great friends afterward, but instead of her chewing me out I chewed her out and told her that she'd got constipated writers."

Woman or no woman, gentleman or no gentleman, you don't tell George Lois what is and isn't "done" without running the risk of a stream of profanity, or worse. This doesn't make him an animal; it makes him passionate about his work. Ron Holland, a copywriter who worked with him for many years, says he is "almost Edwardian in his politeness with people" and he will indeed treat you with a quiet, warm courtesy. Just don't tell him what to do on his layout pad.

When he got Papert's call, Lois didn't linger long. Although being part of the DDB creative department was, as art director Len Sirowitz later said, "like being a team member for the 1927 New York Yankees," the only logical next step was his own shop. And it hadn't escaped his notice that no agency had ever set up with an art director as a partner—he would be the first. He had no doubt they could improve on what Bernbach was doing. His only condition was that he bring his own writer.

LOIS'S FIRST CHOICE was Julian Koenig, white-hot from his almost public fame as the writer of the VW ads. He immediately agreed, for two reasons. First, he'd been knocking around advertising for ten years and he, too, was curious about branching out, to see if he could do it on his own. It was one of those "will I spend the rest of my life wondering?" moments. Second, he had recently experienced an aspect of Bernbach's character that had irritated and annoyed him.

"I wrote an ad for Ancient Age bourbon. Bill went down to the client—copywriters didn't but the account people and Bill went. He came back and stood in the middle of the art department and said, 'They loved my line'. And I said, 'That's my line, not yours'. And he said, 'No, it's my line.' So I called over Bert Steinhauser who I'd done the advert with and said, 'Whose line is this?' and in true heroic form he said, 'I forget.'"

It wasn't an isolated incident. Three years before, in March of 1957, *Time* magazine had published a brief piece on the agency, specifically mentioning Judy Protas as the writer of the Ohrbachs "Cat" ad. Bernbach immediately leaned on the magazine and two weeks later a very similar piece ran which, without direct reference to the issue, made it clear that Bernbach was the author. Although Protas had written the body copy, which is superb, the idea was Bernbach and Gage's. So some of the credit was justified—but was the effort to capture it?

The indignation of the creative people was leavened by the fact that they accepted that as the creator of the environment, Bernbach could claim partial involvement in all their work. (Don Draper makes the same point to Peggy Olson when she complains that he has taken an award for an ad that she wrote.) Even Koenig, irritated as he was, could see Bernbach's position: "Everything in the agency was his. I realize that he thought it was his ad, in the sense that it would not have existed if it had not been for him." But Koenig had also had a run-in over a tire commercial with Joe Daly (the Head of Accounts), and was in a truculent mood.

He went to meet Papert and they immediately recognized each other from the racetrack—four decades later they were still going to the races together—and to a mixture of incredulity and ridicule on the part of the rest of the DDB creative department, the deal was announced.

PAPERT KOENIG LOIS (PKL) opened its doors on the thirty-sixth floor of the Seagram Building on January 1, 1960. The offices had previously been those of Papert & Free, which, coincidentally, Lois had helped them secure a year earlier. Edgar Bronfman of Seagrams had been having trouble letting whole floors as he wanted, and Lois got a tip through Bronfman's son-in-law, a friend of his, that a deal could be struck.

Five people occupied the office on that first day. Says Lois, "I felt off-the-wall excited—and nervous and apprehensive. I didn't know if it was going to work out." Their first client was *The Ladies' Home Journal*, inherited from Papert & Free, quickly followed by Dilly Beans. For these two clients, one staid, one small, they managed to create eye-catching work and they were off and running.

The offices were stylish and hip, the organization cool but chaotic. A visitor once found staff wobbling aimlessly around the office on French Solex motorized bicycles. It looked like a time-and-motion-inspired efficiency initiative; in reality they'd taken on the account and then discovered the bike had no retail outlets in New York. So they decided to become not just advertising agent but dealership as well. It was not a success—no one had bothered to find out that a licence was necessary to ride them on the streets, and the surplus stock ended up in the office.

But within a few months, to give them gravity, they hired an experienced marketing man, Norman Grulich. The agency's work was terrific—possibly even more concentrated than DDB, the ballsy innovative campaigns streamed out and the cream of New York creative talent had a new path to beat. "People wanted to come to us because we were free spirits," says Papert. An ice cream truck driver named Ron Holland decided to switch to a career in advertising based on an ad he saw for Dilly Beans—he wanted to work with people who could write a line as subversive as "If your dealer doesn't stock Dilly Beans, knock something off the shelf as you walk out."

Through Bronfman's company, Seagrams, PKL picked up Wolfschmidt vodka. New Yorkers were startled by a campaign that personified the bottle as a man promiscuously picking his partners from suitable ingredients for a vodka-based cocktail. A vodka bottle flirting with an orange was a long way from the tuxedoed and evening-gowned stiffs that were usually featured in classy alcohol advertisements. It was also, on the threshold of the sixties, deemed a little risqué—*The New Yorker* refused to run the "Who was that tomato I saw you with last night?" version.

Of course, having an ad banned for being risqué, with the notoriety that brought, was meat and drink for the renegade agency. And not all their work was edgy; Koenig was still ever the elegant writer, and Harvey Probber Chairs got the velvety persuasive treatment in an ad whose authorship is still to this day in vigorous dispute between Lois and Koenig.

THE WORK THAT ANNOUNCED their arrival as a fully fledged, grown-up agency capable of handling national brands came about by a succession of lucky bounces.

One Saturday morning after a major snow storm, Fred Papert decided to walk to the office to retrieve the gloves he'd left there the previous evening, towing his kids on a sled behind him. In the brief time they were in the office the phone rang. It was Xerox asking if they'd like to pitch

If your Harvey Probber chair wobbles, straighten your floor.

Every piece of furniture that Harvey Probber makes at Fall River, Mass. is placed on a test platform to make sure it's on the level. If you get it, it is. Mr. Probber loses a lot of furniture this way. Mr. Probber's furniture has an almost luminous satin finish. It is produced by a unique machine that has 5 fingers and is called the human hand.

This luminous finish takes a long time to achieve, but it lasts a long time. The lovely chair above could be made with 14 less dowels, 2 yards less webbing, thinner woods and so forth. You wouldn't know the difference, but Harvey Probber would. Of course, in a few years you would know too. NEW YORK/CHICAGO/DALLAS/BOSTON/ST. LOUIS/MILWAUKEE/NASHVILLE/HARVEY PROBBER DESIGN BOOK; ONE DOLLAR, DEPT. BE20, HARVEY PROBBER, INC., FALL RIVER, MASS.

ABOVE *The disputed Harvey Probber Chair advertisement, created by George Lois and Julian Koenig.*

"You're some tomato.
We could make beautiful Bloody Marys together.
I'm different from those other fellows."

"I like you, Wolfschmidt.
You've got taste."

Wolfschmidt Vodka has the touch of taste that marks genuine old world vodka. Wolfschmidt in a Bloody Mary is a tomato in triumph. Wolfschmidt brings out the best in every drink. General Wine and Spirits Company, N.Y. 22. Made from Grain, 80 or 100 Proof. Prod. of U.S.A.

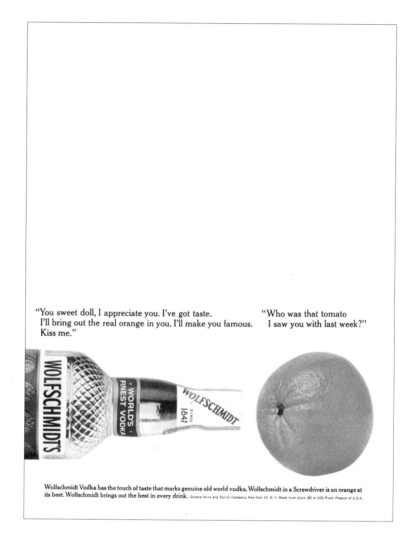

"You sweet doll, I appreciate you. I've got taste. I'll bring out the real orange in you. I'll make you famous. Kiss me."

"Who was that tomato I saw you with last week?"

Wolfschmidt Vodka has the touch of taste that marks genuine old world vodka. Wolfschmidt in a Screwdriver is an orange at its best. Wolfschmidt brings out the best in every drink. General Wine and Spirits Company, New York 22, N. Y. Made from Grain, 80 or 100 Proof. Product of U.S.A.

ABOVE AND OPPOSITE *1960 PKL advertisements for Wolfschmidts, by George Lois and Julian Koenig.*

for the launch of their new photocopier, not a difficult question for Fred to answer. He later learned that one of the reasons they won the business was that Xerox was impressed he was working on such an inclement Saturday morning.

The call itself was also due to fortuitous circumstances. DDB had been offered the business but they couldn't handle it because of conflict with Polaroid—clients have always been hyper paranoid about having their business with an agency that is simultaneously handling a company who could even remotely be considered a rival.

According to Julian Koenig, "Ned Doyle called me up and *sotto voce* told me about an account we might be able to get and says 'but don't tell Bill.'" Xerox had asked Bernbach to give them a list of agencies he would recommend and "he made a list of ten including some quite lugubrious ones, but he omitted us. . . . Bill was an old friend and he would embrace me but he did everything he could not to help. He was offended that we (a) left and (b) succeeded."

Bernbach did have an agenda. Referring to PKL, Bernbach had told Edgar Bronfman, "There's a difference between being smart and smart alec." Bernbach didn't like his children growing up and leaving; when George Gomes, a DDB art director setting out on his own as a commercials director, went to see him to say goodbye, all Bernbach said before he turned his back and walked away was, "Yes, I heard you were leaving." Gomes later heard through former colleagues in the agency that Bernbach had forbidden the department to use him.

There is always the possibility that he genuinely didn't think PKL was right for the job, but if so, in this instance his famed creative radar was out of tune. PKL, and specifically art director Sam Scali and copywriter Michael Chappell, turned in a demonstration commercial about as perfect as can be made. But even in this, fate took a hand.

To illustrate how simple it was to use, they had a small girl make copies on the machine, in real time. It was straightforward, direct, carefully written, and impressive enough to irritate competitors into complaining to the networks that the complexity of operating the machine was being understated. PKL's answer was a typical mixture of belligerence and brilliance; not only did they reshoot the whole commercial, in front of TV executives, but instead of the girl they used a chimpanzee.

ABOVE *The TV "Chimp" advertisement for Xerox: monkey see, monkey do.*

The resulting commercial, with almost no voice-over and the simplest of camera work and editing, is mesmerizing. The chimpanzee is asked by a desk-bound executive—like it happens every day—to make a copy of a document. He takes the document, waddles to the machine, confidently and competently follows the procedure and insouciantly hands the two sheets to the executive, whose only question is "Which one is the original?"

BY 1962 CONFIDENCE was high, billings were at $17 million and, true to their iconoclastic behavior to date, they took one of the most radical steps ever in the history of advertising—they became the first agency to go public. The move was loudly opposed by just about everyone in business. The righteous justification, intoned for public consumption by agency chief after agency chief, was that "we are in the service of our clients, not anonymous shareholders." The real reason was that few successful agencies wanted the balance sheet scrutiny that would necessarily follow the announcement of a flotation.

Agencies were remunerated by a commission from the amount their clients spent on their media exposure, a hangover from the days when their main business was the selling of space. It meant in theory—and very often in practice—they were rewarded for not doing new work; if the same advertisment ran year after year, they would earn their commission for having done nothing more than buy the time or space from the broadcast or print media. It also meant that they had no incentive to keep media expenditure down. On top of that, revenue was bumped up by commission charged on production costs for print and TV executions, as well as on research and other ancillary services. All of which meant these advertising agencies were productive little cash machines from which their owners could withdraw more or less what they wanted, when they wanted it.

Consequently, most of them lived—and rewarded their senior people— far more handsomely than their equivalents at the client companies, something the clients could suspect but never prove. But once you go public, the covers are off.

Fred Papert, whose idea it was, figured he could reward himself and his partners from the pool of wealth that shareholders brought. "Salaries were getting too high—stock was an alternative. It was the route to real wealth, we would have made a fortune." And they weren't yet fat enough to have left any skeletons in their financial cupboard.

Lois articulated a more high-minded motive, albeit in a characteristically abrasive way. He stood received wisdom on its head and claimed that public ownership would make them better partners of their clients. "The concept of public ownership puts us on a par with any company that produces a product. The image of our business no longer has to be that of shufflers who make money because they have a slick line of talk. No pride, just talk."

Despite their howls of protestation, by the end of the decade more than twenty other agencies had sold stock, and five of the top ten were public companies. For PKL, very soon it was seen to be the genesis of the sad, slow disintegration of the agency. Once you have shareholders, you have to deliver to someone else's expectations; doing the work you want to do, regardless of profitability, is no longer viable.

Amongst the influx of clients excited by the freewheeling new agency was the Daddy of them all, then and now, Proctor & Gamble, the undisputed king of packaged goods.

In retrospect it's obvious that P&G, who were always committed to Rosser Reeves' school of advertising, should never have gone to PKL. The last thing they wanted was any sort of originality and certainly not controversy; they wanted only that which had been done a thousand times before, anathema to PKL's founders. But like so many other clients and agencies, they were intrigued by the new creativity and they decided to give the agency a try to see if they were missing something.

It's slightly more forgivable that PKL should have taken the business. There was after all a lot of money and huge credibility to be gained—if you were solid enough for P&G you were solid enough for anyone—and there were now also shareholders to satisfy. They probably made the same mistake as literally hundreds of proudly creative agencies around the world since; that of taking unimaginative left-brained clients in the hope that they would be the ones to tame the beast.

According to Papert, Lois didn't like the idea. "And he was probably right. It made our agency just like any other." All three—Papert, Koenig, and Lois—now say that it was probably the beginning of the end for them.

The cultural fit is so important in a business where no matter how much research you do (and PKL shared DDB's deep suspicion of research), so many creative decisions are simply a matter of opinion. If your judgement derives from a very different outlook than that of your clients, fissures in the relationship will appear very quickly. While the agency respected P&G as a company, they had very little respect for their advertising taste, which was hardly surprising given their showreel. One example of the agency's frustration was to be told they couldn't show a pile of dirty laundry in a Dash soap powder commercial, because it was . . . dirty.

So here we have the excitable Greek art director and the one-time beatnik Jewish copywriter sitting down to discuss ideas with preppy MBAs clothed by Brooks Brothers, whose idea of a creative discussion centered on the color of the dress worn by the obligatory happy housewife in their floor cleaner commercial. "Let's get down on all fours and see this from the client's point of view" was a popular phrase around town.

Defiant words, but as Bob Levenson was to say later when DDB ran into problems with their slice of P&G, "You can't have Proctor & Gamble on your terms. You have Proctor & Gamble on Proctor & Gamble's terms," and that includes careful casting of the people who work on their business.

Papert recalled that though Koenig could be sharp—once at a P&G internal advertising awards ceremony he thanked all of the members of the client team "without whose help the job would have been done a lot quicker"—but he could also be "gentle and nice."

On the other hand, he says of Lois, "George is in your face. He had a problem—he wanted to work on P&G cat food but got asked off. People who like cats don't want smart ass stuff thrown at them." And at PKL it wasn't always just "stuff" that got thrown in your face.

PKL HAD A REPUTATION for brawling. In fact, the agency became known in New York as Stillman's East, after a famous boxing gym on the West Side. As a way of settling differences of opinion, a robust physicality was never far from the surface, even if sometimes it was theatrical, like the occasion when Lois climbed out onto the windowsill of his Matzos client's office and threatened to jump if they didn't buy his ad.

Jerry Della Femina claims that one former writer tried to sue the agency because the atmosphere of intimidation kept him from concentrating on his work. But Lois denies that fighting was an everyday occurrence, even

From left to right: Fred Papert, Julian Koenig, and George Lois. A WASP, a Jew, and a Greek—the prototype sixties Creative Revolution agency.

though he admits to searching for three days for a member of staff who had punched the head of TV: "The guy didn't come in for a week," he growls.

An account handler, Carl Ally, is alleged to have punched George Lois in the stomach. Today, Lois is indignant at the suggestion: "Ally punched me? Are you crazy? I'd have laid him out. It was Papert he went after!"

Illustrating the macho atmosphere at PKL, Lois recalls, "We had the best basketball and softball teams in advertising. Our basketball team played in the Bank league, which had all-American college guys on their teams. The agency was loaded with strong guys. We were all Depression babies, a lot of ethnics, a lot of street kids. It wasn't like walking into an Ogilvy or Benton & Bowles, it was a place where men were men. We'd play in Bedford Stuyvesant where no white people went."

It's sort of appropriate that when it came to doing an ad for their women's fashion store client, Evan-Picone, the models were dressed as mobsters and their molls. It's equally appropriate that the mobsters were Charles Evans, the client; George Lois; an unidentified man from the PKL art studio; and Tony Palladino, an art director at PKL. Later, Palladino was to take the role rather too seriously in an incident in London which today seems comical but at the time was near tragic.

In 1964, PKL had opened an office in London for no particular reason other than that, according to Lois, Papert was an Anglophile and wanted someone to book his West End theater tickets. Two New York PKL staff members were sent over to help set up and run the office: Ron Holland and Tony Palladino. The man appointed to head the Knightsbridge agency was a red-haired, dark-suited English aristocrat, Nigel Seeley (later to become Sir Nigel), a former client of PKL in New York. An ex-army officer, Seeley had been trained in unarmed combat.

Says Peter Mayle, who would become PKL London's creative director, "We all thought he was a toff because he took snuff and his uncle was an earl or a duke. When the uncle died, Nigel inherited the title (and his uncle's crested socks, of which he was sinfully proud). I liked him a lot, I never found him disdainful but he certainly had a patrician manner. This might very easily have upset people."

George Lois, who knew Palladino from childhood, says, "Tony was a tough kid, ready with his dukes. He grew up in East Harlem, black neighborhood. Number of times I'd leave school and find Tony having a fist fight with a couple of black guys. I'd have to drop my books and start swinging."

You can see what's coming. It arrived about an hour before the agency Christmas party. Mayle recalls, "Nigel was in his office having a drink with one of the boys. I don't know what he'd done to infuriate Tony but when he went into Nigel's office it wasn't to wish him Merry Christmas. Strong words must have been exchanged, causing Tony to attack Nigel with a view, or so I heard, to strangling him. Nigel stuck out a hand to defend himself. The hand was holding a glass of champagne. The glass broke off in Tony's neck, not far from the carotid artery. Nigel's hand was also cut open. There was an impressive amount of blood which, as Nigel and Tony moved out of Nigel's office, dripped all over the agency—floor, desks, door handles, account executives' pants, everywhere.

"We spent hours mopping it up, since we had a new business presentation the next morning. Someone had the presence of mind to take Tony to the nearby St. George's hospital and he was never seen in the agency again. I guess that once his wound had been sewn up he got on the first plane to somewhere less violent. Like New York." He had indeed. He was on a flight the next day. It seems that the Stillman's spirit traveled well.

IN 1963, Lois was the New York Art Directors Club Art Director of the Year. Said Herb Lubalin, "Nobody has the right to be so young and so successful." And life was good at PKL. They'd outgrown the Seagram premises and moved to Rockefeller Center, where the key people had offices overlooking the skating rink. One of their growing list of accounts was Restaurant Associates, a company that ran some of the very best eateries in Manhattan, including the hugely fashionable Four Seasons on the ground floor of the Seagram Building. It was practically the agency canteen; Lois, hair slicked back and dressed in one of his uber-sharp Roland Meledandri suits a Madison Avenue tailor whom Lois claims even Ralph Lauren worshipped, had lunch there most days. Top management could eat at whichever of the restaurants they wanted, whenever they wanted, for free. On Saturday nights, Papert and an OB&M copywriter friend Bob Marshall and their wives would see how high they could rack up the bill for dinner; $75 was a satisfying achievement one weekend.

Chaos still reigned. There were, as Papert puts it, "All sorts of internal shenanigans. At one point I got fired—but I just kept coming in. It all blew over." New accounts arrived, often in spite of their best efforts to repel them. At a pitch to National Airlines, the agency showreel was first run backward, and then upside down. In front of an increasingly transfixed client Papert kept up a stream of wisecracks and small talk while the film was reloaded. The projector was ready, the signal was given and the film spooled smoothly all over the floor.

"We just got up and left—what's the point? We were in the car, just about to pull away from the car park and there's a tap on the window. It was Bud Maytag, the National Airlines client. 'OK, we'll do it' he says. 'Do what?' 'We'll give you the business. At least you've demonstrated you're not just slick salesmen.'"

With the problems brought about by the flotation and the tenure of P&G yet to materialize, it didn't matter what the agency did, it worked. Everything was turned on its head. The work you did and the way you did it, the people you hired, the way they behaved, even the way they dressed. If there was a new rule, it was that there were no rules. A new account man, Ted Levinson, on asking for an agenda for a new business meeting was told by Papert (his boss, remember), "Are you kidding? We don't do agendas." There was a new pride—the obsequious ad hustler was dead. In his place was the assertive new ad man who would happily tell you that you may know all about your product, but don't even think about telling him anything about advertising.

Account executive Phil Sussbrick was with Lois at Quaker Oats in Chicago presenting some new ads when Lois got to one of which he was particularly proud. Sussbrick was appalled—but not particularly surprised—to hear him preface the layout with, "And if you don't buy this, you can kiss my ass." Then he thought again, changed his mind and said, "No, you can kiss Sussbrick's ass."

In Jerry Della Femina's memoir he writes of a joke circulating Madison Avenue featuring the switchboard operators of various agencies. There were many variations, characterizing the way the business was evolving.

"Good morning, this is Ogilvy and Mather—how can we oblige?"

"DDB, Shalom."

"This is PKL—who the fuck are you?"

7 Avis v Hertz

"We're all here because of you.
Everything we do is to please you."

PEGGY OLSEN TO DON DRAPER MAD MEN

Within the overall discipline that all advertising exists only to sell and everything else was secondary, the creative people at DDB were given complete freedom of the lay-out pad. During a 1965 interview on life at DDB, copywriter Ron Rosenfeld likened the agency to Summerhill, a leading progressive school in England. It was a touching analogy. Summerhill was almost free of rules, with a philosophy that allowed children to experience their full range of feelings. The school accepted that the freedom the children were given to make their own decisions always involved risk, and so allowed for mistakes to be made.

This was eerily reflective of Bernbach's attitude at DDB, and the fully-grown and otherwise hard-bitten creative people were almost dizzy with adulation of their teacher.

"We were working for the approval of one person—Bill Bernbach," says art director Bob Kuperman. "To get your ad pinned up on his 'Best of the Month' board, they wanted that more than anything, more than any awards. They were only juries. But this was Bernbach."

"We did it to see Bill's eyes light up," said Bob Gage.

This near self-abasement had its material consequences. DDB were dreadful paymasters, knowing that people would take a cut in salary to work there. Kuperman turned down an offer from Delehanty, Kurnit &

Geller that would have tripled his salary. Later in the sixties, when the size borne of its very success became the seed of its own slow decline and DDB lost some of its passion, the creative people were surprised by how far they'd fallen behind in the salaries they could command.

But for the time being they didn't care. In return for their cultish submission within the Church of Bernbach they were granted holy status without. If you worked for DDB you moved in rarefied air, and you knew it. Jim Raniere, an art director, remembered the parties that production companies would throw around Christmas and holidays: "You go into this huge room with all the advertising people in New York going to dance and eat and Doyle Dane used to stand to one side, not mixing. I think we were, at that time, a little self-involved. Well, we were doing the work so we felt we were different from the way they were doing it."

The work continued to dazzle. Coffee of Colombia was sold with bonhomie through a good-natured fictitious coffee grower, Juan Valdez. A campaign was created for the Jamaica Tourist Board that was as literary and elegant as anything Ogilvy had ever written for the British Tourist Authority. Some of the sly wit of Orbach's and VW showed through in a Chivas Regal campaign of such clever conviction that it turned an ordinary whisky into, in its own unashamed words, the "Chivas Regal of Whiskies."

THE NEXT CAMPAIGN to attract the same attention and admiration as Volkswagen was Avis. Robert "Bob" Townsend, a former American Express executive, had been appointed by banker Lazard Freres in a last ditch attempt to save the ailing car rental company, which had been leaching money for eleven consecutive years. His approach was about as unconventional as his eventual advertising.

As Clive Challis reports in *Helmut Krone. The Book*, "Townsend dispensed with a secretary, fired the Avis public relations department, insisted that management undergo the same training as the field staff, cut meeting times by insisting that everybody stand up throughout them, and later wrote the bestseller *Up the Organization*. [It] went into several reprints and became something of a handbook for an alternative management style."

When he called Bernbach to outline his problem and asked how they would work together, the answer he got was so extraordinary that Townsend wrote it down.

"What you do is let us have ninety days to learn your business, and then you run every ad where we tell you to put it and just as we write it. You don't change a thing." He then urged Townsend to call all DDB's existing clients for a recommendation and that was it—The Presentation. Take it or leave it. Townsend couldn't resist.

The writer assigned to the business was Paula Green. Born in California in 1927, she'd come to New York and got a job as secretary to the promotions manager of *True*, a men's magazine. He involved her in every aspect of magazine production, including writing. When he left she took his job but then went on to join the promotions department of Grey advertising, where she could write full time.

By 1956, DDB was already becoming an interesting agency and as she'd met Ned Doyle at Grey she gave him a call. He arranged for her to come in to meet Phyllis Robinson, after which she was hired. She was teamed up with Helmut Krone with whom she'd never been paired before. The relationship was not always harmonious—Green at one time threatened to resign over Krone's attempt at "improving" her copy—but between them they produced a campaign every bit as radical and successful as Krone and Koenig's VW work.

It was not dissimilar—candor was its heart, its impact, and its leverage. The opening layouts were a direct reversal of the VW layout: big headlines and copy, small picture. There was one radical advertising departure— there was no logo. Krone predicted that the consistency of the distinctive look would bring brand recognition, and he was right.

As with the VW campaign, the agency capitalized on Avis's immediate apparent disadvantages. Far from hiding the fact that they were a distant second to Hertz in size, the team turned it into a potential benefit to the user. In the very first ad they asked the question, "Avis is only No. 2 in rent a cars. So why go with us?" The answer was the campaign theme: "We try harder."

To conventional contemporary advertising eyes "We're No. 2" was a shocking misjudgement, a page one error. Indeed, it failed research tests—50 percent of respondents said they didn't want to be associated

ABOVE *Bottled sophistication; the Chivas Regal campaign by DDB ran from 1963 to 1970.*

Avis can't afford unwashed cars.

Or smudged mirrors, dirty ashtrays, or anything less than new cars like lively, super-torque Fords.
Why?
When you're not the biggest in rent a cars, you have to try harder.
We do.
We're only No. 2.

The writer of this ad rented an Avis car recently. Here's what I found:

Cigarette butts. A whole ashtray full.

I write Avis ads for a living. But that doesn't make me a paid liar.
When I promise that the least you'll get from Avis is a clean Plymouth with everything in perfect order, I expect Avis to back me up.
I don't expect full ashtrays; it's not like them.
I know for a fact that everybody in that company, from the president down, tries harder.
"We try harder" was their idea; not mine.
And now they're stuck with it; not me.
So if I'm going to continue writing these ads, Avis had better live up to them. Or they can get themselves a new boy.
They'll probably never run this ad.

If you have a complaint, call the president of Avis. His number is CH 8-9150.

If he doesn't answer after I rings, try later.

There isn't a single secretary to protect him. He answers the phone himself.
He's a nut about keeping in touch. He believes it's one of the big advantages of a small company.
You know who is responsible for what. There's nobody to pass the buck to.
One of the frustrations of complaining to a big company is finding someone to blame.
Well, our president feels responsible for the whole kit and caboodle. He has us working like crazy to keep our super-torque Fords super. But he knows there will be an occasional dirty ashtray or temperamental wiper.
If you find one, call our president collect.
He won't be thrilled to hear from you, but he'll get you some action.

No. 2ism. The Avis Manifesto.

We are in the rent a car business, playing second fiddle to a giant.
Above all, we've had to learn how to stay alive.
In the struggle, we've also learned the basic difference between the No. 1's and No. 2's of the world.
The No. 1 attitude is: "Don't do the wrong thing. Don't make mistakes and you'll be O.K."
The No. 2 attitude is: "Do the right thing. Look for new ways. Try harder."
No. 2ism is the Avis doctrine. And it works.
The Avis customer rents a clean, new Plymouth, with wipers wiping, ashtrays empty, gas tank full, from an Avis girl with smile firmly in place.
And Avis itself has come out of the red into the black. Avis didn't invent No. 2ism. Anyone is free to use it.
No. 2's of the world, arise!

Avis is only No.2 in rent a cars. So why go with us?

We try harder.

(When you're not the biggest, you have to.)

We just can't afford dirty ash-trays. Or half-empty gas tanks. Or worn wipers. Or unwashed cars. Or low tires. Or anything less than seat-adjusters that adjust. Heaters that heat. Defrost-ers that defrost.

Obviously, the thing we try hardest for is just to be nice. To start you out right with a new car, like a lively, super-torque Ford, and a pleasant smile. To know, say, where you get a good pastrami sandwich in Duluth.

Why?

Because we can't afford to take you for granted.

Go with us next time.

The line at our counter is shorter.

ABOVE AND OPPOSITE *The Avis campaign by DDB (1962–66), created by art director Helmut Krone, and with copywriters such as Paula Green and David Herzbrun.*

with anything except number one. But Bernbach said it should run anyway; he argued that while "We're No. 2" had the more immediate impact, the irrefutable follow up logic of "We try harder" would soon become convincing.

The impact was undeniable. Fred Danzig, then a reporter on *Ad Age*, recalls that the opening ad came into the office on a Friday "and broke as a Last Minute News item in that Monday's issue. I remember how we gathered around the ad and simply went nuts . . . the audacity, the originality, the freshness, the life, the sassy spirit. . . . It forever changed the way Madison Avenue—and the rest of us—communicated to the world.'

With short succinct copy, a succession of ads made the same point. As an idea, it was more than an advertising promise. By publicly claiming, and committing, to "We try harder," the service staff at Avis had to follow up. The organization was dragged, almost shamed, into higher service levels by its advertising. In 1963, when the campaign started, Avis revenues were $35 million. The next year they were $44 million. To Townsend's credit, a $3.2 million loss was turned into a $3 million profit in a single year.

For DDB, honesty was clearly proving the best policy and at times the candor was absolute, as on the occasion when David Herzbrun and Helmut Krone sampled the Avis offering for a trip out to the company's Garden City headquarters. They were less than impressed with the rental car they were given and in two days produced the ad shown on the next page:

"The writer of this ad rented an Avis car recently. Here's what I found:"

Townsend hated it. According to Herzbrun, "It went against everything he believed about how to do advertising. It was negative. It kept on being negative. 'Right', we said. 'And we want to run it.'"

A compromise was reached. They could run it as long as they told him exactly where and when it was going to appear, so he could make sure he never saw it again.

Townsend himself took the trying harder promise to its limit. One ad headlined his real phone number for anyone with a complaint to ring him personally. In the history of service business it's difficult to imagine an example of a CEO demonstrating his commitment in a more direct way.

With Hertz publicly targeted in all but name there was bound to be an impact on the Number 1, but that was not necessarily Avis's aim. They were just as happy to sweep up the custom from their competitors in third, fourth, and fifth place, increasing their market share as number two. But it was hurting Hertz enough that by 1966 they felt they had to do something about it.

They called Carl Ally Inc.

CARL ALLY OPENED for business in Manhattan on June 25, 1962. He was an account man, but not as anyone knew them, then or since. Amil Gargano, Ally's business partner for the best part of thirty years, describes the account people of the era as "the Captains. They were the brass of the agency business and that's how they conducted themselves. They never took their jackets off, their sleeves were never rolled up, their ties were always straight. They were incredibly boring—and then in comes one with his shirt tails out, his fly open, his tie loose, his hair mussed up. . . . An English major from Michigan who would quote Shakespeare and swear like a longshoreman in the same sentence. . . . An incredibly colorful person—and people were captivated."

Five foot seven, stockily built, and pugnacious, Carl Ally (or the Terrible Turk as he liked to call himself) was born in Detroit in 1924 to an Italian-American mother and a Turkish father. A fighter pilot in Europe in World War II and in Korea, winning both a Distinguished Flying Cross and a Presidential Citation, he never quite left the barrack room behind, despite his searing articulacy and intellect. Erwin Ephron, a media department head, remembers Ally's short but devastating analysis to Hugh Hefner after a long, high-minded presentation on the quality of *Playboy* magazine's original fiction: "Fine Hef—but take the tits out and see what happens." A young copywriter, proudly showing the first cut of a commercial with an elaborate narrative obscuring the sales message, was urged to re-edit with the terse critique "too much foreplay and not enough fucking."

After Korea he went into advertising in a small Detroit agency before moving to Campbell Ewald, a bigger outfit made grand by its tenure of the General Motors account. But it wasn't long before he had one eye on the bigger opportunities for both him and the agency in their tiny New York office and he short-circuited the process of getting transferred with a startling piece of initiative.

While on vacation in Manhattan, he read in *The New York Times* that the Swissair business was up for grabs. He contacted them, got the agency on their pitch list, made the presentation single-handedly and won the account. The first the Detroit management knew the account was loose was when Ally called them to tell them they'd won it.

Impressed, they agreed he should be based in New York permanently, not just for servicing Swissair but to expand the office.

The New York office was a sleepy hollow; a handful of functionaries going through the motions of handling a few quiet local offshoots of GM business. But Ally shook it up. He was, as Amil Gargano wrote in his book about the agency, *Ally and Gargano*, "an earthquake in a nursing home," literally moving into the office and sleeping in a sleeping bag.

THE FIRST HELP ALLY needed was creative so he asked for James Durfee and Amil Gargano, a copywriter and an art director he'd worked with back in Detroit. Ironically for Durfee, he'd joined Campbell Ewald only because his previous agency, JWT Detroit, had wanted to transfer him to New York and he hadn't liked the idea. But with his second New York offer in a year, he decided that fate was trying to tell him something and this time he agreed to move.

Amil Gargano was more than ready to go. Born in Detroit on June 4, 1932 to Italian immigrant parents, he showed early promise as an illustrator and entered the world of advertising as a paste-up artist at Campbell Ewald. Within just six months Gargano had been promoted to assistant art director.

Two years later, an art director new to the agency introduced Gargano to the New York Art Directors Club awards annual. It was an epiphany. For the first time he saw advertisments for Levy's and Orbach's and the work of Bob Gage, and that was when he asked for a transfer to the only place he wanted to be—New York. Ally's Swissair win made that move possible, and in April 1959, Ally, Gargano and Durfee were together for the first time in Manhattan.

Ally quickly added to the Swissair win. His high-profile air force presence in the two wars resulted not only in the belief that he was the model for Yossarian from *Catch 22* (a story promoted largely by himself

ABOVE *Carl Ally as a fighter pilot in Europe during World War II. Attitude? What does it look like?*

but credible to those who knew him), but also in a huge contact list in the aviation business. Those contacts helped in the subsequent gain of the United Aircraft Corporation (UAC) account.

His vibrant and usually oath-laden style was clearly paying off. But not everyone was finding Ally's exuberance and energy infectious. Problems on Swissair and United Aircraft, clients that the company wouldn't even have had if it hadn't been for him, had ruffled the feathers of the top management. First, they objected to him taking Gargano and Durfee on a fact-finding trip to Switzerland, seeing no reason why he couldn't go alone and brief the creatives on his return. (This was the same year several DDB staffers, creative people included, were making trips back and forth to Wolfsburg, Germany to learn about VW.)

Second, United Aircraft had not liked the campaign prepared for them and Ally was seeking the assistance of the Detroit management in getting it through. Instead, they backed UAC and, to the huge relief of the previous regime at the New York office, Carl Ally's charismatic but disruptive spell in New York crashed and burned just two weeks before Christmas 1959, when he was summoned to Detroit and fired on the spot.

Shocked, dismayed, and disgusted with the management, Gargano made every attempt to get out, but the only place he really wanted to work was DDB and they wouldn't even see his book, let alone him. He was stuck. Durfee, married with a child and living in Connecticut, had even less flexibility.

After a year without work, Ally was close to a breakdown. He was on the verge of going back to Detroit and starting over when Gargano suggested he talk to the lively new PKL, thinking it would be a meeting of minds—or at least attitudes. And he wasn't wrong. George Lois recalls, "Account guys bored me, they were full of shit but when I met Carl Ally, I said, 'Gee, the guy's got blood running through his veins.'" He thinks for a second and then adds, "Amazing that I liked him—he was a Turk and I'm a Greek!"

Ally was in his element, established in the sort of New York organization he'd originally envisaged. "Wings and wheels" being his forte throughout his life, he was happy on various automotive accounts, particularly Peugeot, but he became increasingly dissatisfied with his remuneration and particularly the partners' refusal to allow him any company stock. So in April 1962, when his Peugeot client, Jim LaMarre, told him he was leaving to take up the job of marketing director at Volvo, Ally seized the opportunity and convinced LaMarre to allow him to pitch for the business with a new agency he would form around the account.

Durfee had by now moved back to semi-familiar turf at JWT New York, Gargano to B&B, but in nine months he hadn't had a single piece of work published and when Ally approached them with the idea of forming an agency, both were ready to go for it.

They worked on the pitch after their normal working day. And, despite the fact that the limited resources and cramped timeframe caused the layouts to carry the brand name misspelt as "Valvo" (Ally being Ally, some recollections inevitably have it as "Vulva"), they won the business.

GARGANO AND DURFEE are both mild-mannered, civilized, considered men. Even allowing for youthful brashness, they were a direct contrast to the pugnacious, occasional combatative style of their colleague. But together they created a campagin for Volvo that was probably the most confrontational—literally—in the history of US advertising to date. Until then, any product comparison in advertising was by implication only, and you never ever named the competition. Yet right from the start, in commercials and print ads, they not only named competitive cars but showed them as well.

The campaign had the same frank freshness of VW. Ad after ad reiterated the Volvo's rugged construction and longevity, while ridiculing Detroit's built-in obsolescence, which made the Volvo not the aspirational choice or the stylish choice or the sexy or high-performance choice—it made it the clever choice.

Following Volvo was another candid and compelling campaign for the New York Automat chain, Horn and Hardart. As pioneer fast-food restaurants, the high quality of their food was belied by the basic surroundings. Simple meals, prepared fresh on the premises, were placed in small glass-fronted display boxes, released by dropping a nickel in the slot. It was low-budget eating but the advertising never claimed anything else. Quite the reverse, in fact—it claimed that the money saved on pretentious surroundings and elaborate service went on the one thing you'd want—good food.

ABOVE *The Carl Ally campaign for Horn & Hardart;*
a lesson in clarity and candor from Ed McCabe.

The campaign was written by a punchy, young Irish-American copywriter, Ed McCabe. From an underprivileged Irish background and a tough upbringing in Chicago, he left school at the age of fifteen and took a variety of jobs. One of these was in an advertising agency, where he'd noticed that the copywriters seemed to do the least work and have the most fun, so that's what he decided he wanted to do. He started writing spec ads in his spare time and getting them in front of as many people as possible. With that dedication he worked his way into a copywriting job at McCann Erikson Chicago in 1954, then on to New York in 1959, where he started at Benton & Bowles on the same day as Gargano.

As with Gargano, B&B's old school style frustrated McCabe and he joined Carl Ally within a year of the start up. He eventually became the youngest copywriter ever elected to the One Club Hall of Fame.

His style is simultaneously direct and disarmingly conversational, writing with wonderful clarity. In contrast with the WASP copywriters of old, he spun the lines with tremendous energy and impact using vernacular and slang. For some, McCabe is the copywriter's copywriter.

WITH CHARACTERISTIC PRIDE Ally would say, "At DDB they like to goose the consumer—but at Carl Ally Inc we punch them on the nose," appropiate from a man who once told a meeting of the Volvo sales force "You guys couldn't sell c*** in a lumberyard." And, from Hertz's point of view, it wasn't just the consumer that needed the punch, it was Avis.

So when representatives from Hertz called Carl Ally Inc to help them attack the Avis campaign they couldn't have made a better choice. As the Ally presentation team told them, "You're getting your asses kicked and it's time to kick back." Between 1963 and 1966 Avis's market share had risen from 29 percent to 36 percent and Hertz had fallen from 61 to 49 percent. It's not too fanciful to suggest that, given another three years, Hertz could have been "Only No. 2" and having to try very much harder themselves.

With a licence to get down and dirty, Durfee and Gargano were acutely aware that the world (well, the ad world at least) would be watching with more than usual interest. Responding directly to a rival in public in any

ABOVE *From left to right: Art director Amil Gargano, copywriter Jim Durfee and Carl Ally.*

field is often unwise and always highly delicate. The slightest false note could make you look petulant, worried or even downright rude. And even though Avis had started the fight, it was easier to be them. Everyone loves an underdog.

The looming rumble was going to be a spectacle for the ad business and all the heavyweights of the trade were filling the ringside seats, waiting for the initial counterpunch from Hertz. The team knew they had to be firm, but cool and confident, as befits a market leader.

Says Amil, describing an internal meeting to discuss the opening salvo, "Jim and I had put together a couple of pretty tough layouts . . . but we couldn't get the first ad right. During a brief moment when the room went silent, John [Carpender, the account supervisor] spoke up. 'Hey, what if we say 'For years Avis has been telling you Hertz is number one'?"

"Durfee finished the headline, '. . . now we're going to tell you why.'"

And that's precisely what Durfee and Gargano did. Hertz, aloof for four years, now reminded the customer why they'd got to number one in the first place—more outlets, more and better cars, money-back satisfaction guarantees, a hotline— and all with the sort of fond but crushing put-down from an older brother to a noisy sibling.

It was aggressive—but its good humor alleviated any nastiness. By playing Avis on their own turf, they even admitted to occasional mistakes, like an ad in which the only visual was an open ashtray with a single cigarette butt in it. Underneath there was a candid admission of infrequent failure, but only after a devastatingly precise demolition of Avis's weaknesses. The barrage was relentless—it was always civil but never without the iron fist.

After the initial burst, a TV commercial by Ed McCabe and an elegant young art director, Ralph Ammirati, showed the air slowly leaking out of one of the ubiquitous "We try harder" Avis balloons while the voice-over ran through the litany of Avis shortcomings. As the recitation nears its end, so does the air in the balloon, escaping with an increasingly irreverent farting noise. "Hertz regrets that we had to do this in public—but it had to be done."

The same team, under the headline "Aha! You were expecting another get tough with Avis ad," showed a smiling Hertz counter assistant patting a happy Avis girl who can't see what the reader can—how cruelly she's being patronized. Helmut Krone cited that specific ad as the beginning of the end for Avis and DDB. "Bernbach came in after McCabe's first ad ran and threw *The New York Times* down on my desk: 'Have you seen this? Don't tell me how bad you think it is. As of today, they are alive—and we just died. What are you going to do about it?'"

Good question. Hertz and Carl Ally had put them in a difficult position. Nothing that they were saying could be refuted, and retaliating would probably only turn what had been an engaging spectator sport into an undignified public squabble. DDB did try, with a couple of half-hearted ads. Ally replied just once and then, amid some accusation from the industry that it had become more about the two agencies yelling at each other than trying to shift a client's product, Hertz moved on to a more assertive and positive campaign. DDB, too, abandoned "We try harder" only ninety days after the Hertz campaign broke. After a change of ownership at Avis, they lost the account.

Oddly, both campaigns can justifiably claim success. For four years DDB had markedly improved Avis's share, but then Hertz's campaign froze their relative positions. Both campaigns had opened new ways in which companies could compete, not just in the market place, but in the media. For Carl Ally, Hertz confirmed the company in the same way that VW had confirmed DDB.

Carl Ally Inc was now properly established, a third front after DDB and PKL in the revolutionary war. It became another aspirational destination for creative people with new ideas. Stories of the wild and often lascivious behavior of its paunchy, rumpled leader—Gargano can't be certain he ever saw Ally with his shirt properly tucked in, no matter how elevated the occasion—delighted and appalled New York, possibly attracting creatives as much as the work.

HELAYNE SPIVAK, a secretary turned writer who eventually became creative director of Y&R, remembers being grabbed by Ally who happily "rammed his tongue down my throat, right there by my desk. The others must have taken him aside and said, 'Look Carl, you can't go on like this and you've got to go and apologize to Helayne.'"

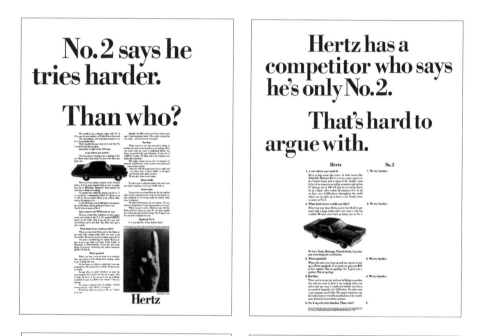

No.2 says he tries harder.

Than who?

Hertz has a competitor who says he's only No.2.

That's hard to argue with.

If you were in the car rental business and you were No.2 and you had only half as many cars to offer and about half as many locations at which to offer them, and fewer people to handle everything, what would you say in your advertising?

Right. Your ashtrays are cleaner.

Hertz
(Who's perfect?)

Aha!
You were expecting another get tough with Avis ad.

She giggles as she tells it. "So he came up to me and by way of apology—
he did it again! I suppose I should have been upset but somehow, it didn't
really offend; it was Carl, I guess, it was just the way he was."

Another secretary, Pat Sutula (later Langer), who also became a writer,
remembers an all-staff memo from Ally announcing yet another party on
some puny pretext. "It ended 'I want you all there—remember, there's
still three of you I haven't yet had,' and I thought, Oh my God, I've only
been here three weeks, he must mean me!"

This is monstrous by today's standards, but he carried it off. Even though
the agency ended in fractiousness in the 1980s, affection for the man was
enormous and lasted his lifetime. Marsha Cohen, who worked with him in
the eighties, said, "He had a very distinctive flat, Midwestern accent, very
noticeable to a New Yorker—he did not sound like the rest of us, that's
for sure. So even though he said irreverant things and cursed like a
sailor . . . there was a little of the hick in him, which I think probably
softened the expletives."

His huge appetite for fun and adventure (he was never far from a party
and never without an aircraft of some sort to fly himself to meetings
whenever possible), and his passion for the work and for "his people,"
endeared him to the staff.

One of the more radical ideas was the year-round four-day week,
designed to give the staff longer leisure breaks. To reassure clients that
their agency wasn't slacking, it was policed vigorously and Ally insisted
that people worked thirty-six hours minimum each week.

It started as an experiment, and when it was confirmed a T-shirt for the
staff was produced featuring a sketch of Ally and the words, "First, Fridays
Off. Now, Free Underwear."

It's difficult to imagine Reeves, Ogilvy or Bernbach doing that, or their
staff being anything other than embarrassed by it. But it was so different
at Carl Ally Inc.

8 Changing Times

' I've got a friend at an agency – I can't say which one – all they do all day long is sit around and smoke mary jane.'

PAUL KINSEY TO PEGGY OLSEN **MAD MEN**

In a recollection of his days at the New York office of Campbell Ewald, Amil Gargano noted the gulf between the Old and the New. Their offices at 488 Madison Avenue were one floor above the establishment Norman, Craig & Kummel agency.

"I would see Norman B. Norman, wearing a Chesterfield topcoat, fedora, a long-stemmed pipe tightly gripped in his jaw, moving in long strides through the lobby to enter his vintage Rolls Royce, his driver dutifully standing at kerb side with his hand on the open rear door. I remember thinking how out of touch one of us must have been."

Creative people were still dressing smartly for business but the preppy style was retreating before the sharper elegance that was flooding into the business with the younger, less reverential breed. In a 1964 ad in an advertising trade magazine, a stock photo library service, ran an ad showing sixteen smartly-attired art directors—none of them had dressed in a particularly special style for the shoot. They are all of Italian origin, the "Graphic Mafia" as photographer Carl Fischer called them. By today's standards the ad is breathtakingly politically incorrect. Under the headline "Are Italian art directors more creative?", came the offer "This week only, special discount for Italian art directors on Wide World's file of 50 million photos."

There was, of course, uproar from every non-Italian. Staged or real, the upshot was that after a complaint by Lou Dorfsman at CBS on behalf of Jewish art directors, the offer was extended to all. Although the flags of neither Helmut Krone nor George Lois had been represented in this global bunfight, one way or another the ethnics had arrived and were hogging the spotlight.

DDB was very much still the beacon on the hill for all creative people, but internally it was a dull, almost dowdy environment where the staff largely kept their heads down and got on with the job. "But at the same time, it wasn't a monastery; there were shenanigans going on, screwing on desks and people being sick in their waste baskets," says Kuperman reassuringly.

JOE DALY, the head of account management, was in some ways a clone of Ned Doyle: Irish, charismatic, hard drinking, and hard living. After Fordham University and war service as a much decorated fighter pilot at Guadalcanal and Midway on the USS *Enterprise,* he joined DDB in 1959 just a few months after it was founded. He made his mark, becoming president in 1968 and CEO in 1976. As the lead executive on the Polaroid and Avis accounts he was one of the most colorful leaders the agency ever had, and he was utterly dedicated to his clients. A colleague once said that if Daly ever became president of the United States, his first loyalty would still be to Polaroid.

He was also a womanizer, another thing he had in common with Doyle. According to Doris Willens, "Stewardesses of American Airlines, one of Daly's major accounts, and the scrubbed blonde demonstrators at Polaroid conventions were among Daly's favorite targets. . . . Daly's wife vented her anger one night by piling all his suits into a bathtub and running steaming hot water until they shrank beyond salvation."

But in this area of expertise even Daly was outplayed by the older Doyle, as Daly himself once acknowledged: "He'd go up to a women and say, 'Hey, you' and pop! I tell you, that guy was very, very wicked with women." Both men slowly lost the respect of the morally-grounded Bernbach, but Daly would regularly redeem himself at early morning meetings even after a long night of licentious excess.

At every level there has always been a certain amount of what Joy Golden, a writer who started at BBDO in 1952, calls "a little nonsense at the office" but, she adds, "nothing like as bad as in *Mad Men*." One of the key factors influencing social behavior in that era was the 1960 legalization of the contraceptive pill and the resulting sexual liberation, although the more libidinous behavior was not the province of ad people alone. This was also the year of Billy Wilder's *The Apartment*, in which a clerk climbs the corporate ladder in exchange for allowing senior executives the use of his apartment to take their girlfriends. It could have been Sterling Cooper—but it was set in a life insurance office.

DRINKING ON AGENCY premises was comparatively rare, although not unknown. It was rumored that some OB&M executives would smuggle lunchtime drinks into the office from Rattazzi's, across the road. They did so to liven up the bland fare served in the cafeteria, installed by Ogilvy himself in the clearly futile attempt to stop his employees drinking alcohol at lunchtime.

Dick Rattazzi, the former *maître d'* at the showbiz restaurant Sardis, had opened his dimly lit two-floored restaurant at 9 East Forty-eighth Street in May 1956. It became such a noisy media haunt in the sixties that a group of ad agency people who practically lived there had a plaque erected outside the premises, in celebration of its notoriety as a Madison Avenue joint.

On West Fifty-second Street, in the former speakeasy 21, Rosser Reeves would be at his regular table eating his habitual corned beef hash, the surrounding tables packed with ad people. They thronged the pavements of Forty-sixth Street between Eighth and Ninth Avenue, "Restaurant Row" as it became known, while Tehran was a popular hang-out for the DDB crowd. Ted Shaine, a DDB art director, remembers noisy gatherings in the Mens Bar at the long-gone Biltmore Hotel at Grand Central Station. "It was like a club. There was a room there where you could actually mix your own martinis and I guess after one or two things could get a little sloppy. You could get food there but no one went there to eat. I ordered a salad once and everyone stood round, poking it—'what's that?' It was a great institution."

He also recalls a bar called Cheetah, a forerunner of the legendary Studio 54 of the seventies and eighties. "It was right near the Fifty-ninth Street Bridge. It was phenomenal, there was a house band, not DJs like now, but there was music and dancing. I'm talking '64 to '67. We'd work very hard all day and then go out all night. It was an amazing time."

ONE MAN WHO LIVED THE LIFE was Jerry Della Femina, a Brooklyn-born college dropout. While he was working as a messenger boy in the late 1950s delivering to advertising agencies, he was attracted to the job of copywriter as "they didn't look like they were working." After several years hawking his book of sample ads he had created in his spare time, he finally got a job in 1961 at Daniel & Charles, a small Jewish run agency.

Within a year he was fired. He had set up a freelance creative consultancy using Daniel & Charles' address on his letterhead, and in error sent a soliciation to one of their clients. But this was a time of full employment, jobs were plentiful, and he quickly found another at DK&G, one of the agencies attempting to follow in DDB's creative footsteps.

Here he gained his first piece of notoriety when he managed to feature a nude woman—in an ad for a foot ointment. Next he won several awards for work on Talon Zippers. Although he himself would admit the campaign had been running for some years before he was assigned to it, his executions were noticeably witty, fun, and daring—not unlike the fellow himself.

Outrageous behavior, good-natured controversy, and ribald laughter accompanied this bald bear of a man wherever he went. His next move, to Bates along with three other creative people from DK&G, was one of those controversies. Bates was still at the opposite end of the prevailing creative mood and represented the worst of the stuff-shirted old world that Jerry and his ilk were fast shucking off. But there was a scheming method in this seeming madness. He knew they would pay him good money because they valued him as an energetic high-profile Italian writer who could help them appear sexier. And he knew he could learn from them.

The Achilles heel of the new creative agencies—and even, to a certain extent, of Ogilvy—was creating advertising for packaged goods, those low-priced, fast-moving grocery items that are the backbone of everyday marketing. The newer agencies were terrific at communicating the values of luxury goods or items with a more considered purchase, like cars or clothing, but a "creative" answer to the challenge of selling a soap powder or a cake mix had so far largely eluded them. Della Femina figured that if he could combine the Bates USP style of work for products like M&Ms and Anacin with the new, more street wise approaches, he could mold a new way of advertising for even the most mundane of products.

But he also used Bates as a publicity platform for the next step in his career, upping his profile further by making speeches and writing articles that were often unapproved, and sometimes even in contradiction of views held by the Bates management. After one such speech, he phoned Fred Danzig, a reporter at *Advertising Age* from 1962 until his retirement as Editor in 1994, and told him that he was in deep trouble with Archie Forster, the head of Bates, and was going to be fired.

"So that Monday in *Ad Age*, [he ran the] headline, 'Della Femina to be fired'. I got called down by Forster. He was an old Southerner and he said, 'What are we going to do with you, boy?' And I said, 'Well, Archie, if you read *Ad Age* today you are probably going to fire me.' He said, 'I can't fire you when you say you are going to be fired! . . . You bought yourself some time didn't you, boy?' I said, 'Yeah, I guess I did.' I knew I was going to start my own agency anyway. I just needed that time. I did a lot of work for Bates on Panasonic and I learned a lot there. It was a great education."

IT WAS WHILE WORKING on Panasonic that he came up with one of the most famous lines in advertising history, more so even than "Think Small" or "Lemon." His suggestion was unveiled to an internal meeting of senior Bates executives who were struggling to find a solution to selling Japanese electronics products less than twenty years after the end of the war in the Pacific. They all leaned forward eagerly when their expensive new star copywriter solemnly announced, "Gentlemen, I have it." There was a gasp of horror as he unveiled: "From those wonderful folks who brought you Pearl Harbor."

It was never seriously intended; there's a tradition in advertising of writing outrageous ads that could never run. Often, they're the first flights of fancy by a creative team when they initially get the brief—they

ABOVE AND OPPOSITE *Jerry Della Femina gained attention and awards for his work on Talon Zippers ads while at DK&G.*

A prominent New York stockbroker just went public.

It's bad enough when the market takes a sudden plunge.

But when your trouser zipper goes down, you lose another kind of security. So for your own good, look for the Talon Zephyr® nylon zipper next time you buy yourself a suit or a pair of slacks.

The Zephyr zipper is designed not to snag, or jam. And a little device called Memory Lock® will make sure your zipper stays up.

So all you'll have to worry about going down are your stocks.

get all of the cynicism and the ribaldry out of the way before they knuckle down to the task. Bob Olsen got a copywriter job from Phyllis Robinson on the strength of a campaign that never ran. The line was, "If it isn't Wolfschmidt's Vodka, it isn't breakfast." David Herzbrun, with George Lois, wrote a headline for Lanteen Diaphragms and Vaginal Gel: "Lanteen: Fecund to None." Both Della Femina and Carl Ally lay claim to the unsurprisingly never-used line for Preparation H, a haemorrhoids treatment: "Up yours with ours—and kiss your piles goodbye." The Pearl Harbor line was used, and to great effect, although not to sell televisions or stereos. Della Femina made it the title of his memoir and it sold many thousands of copies.

DELLA FEMINA WAS thirty-one, and his partner Ron Travisano twenty-nine, when they opened their eponymous agency in 1967. From day one it was unlike anything anyone had ever seen before. Jerry himself said in a *Fortune* interview in April 1987, "My management skills aren't as good as they should be. Heaven knows what's happening on my watch."

What was happening was, in the words of art director Ted Shaine, "like Woodstock—without the mud. It was a party the whole time." Bob Kuperman, who went there as creative director in 1968, said, "We did do some work but it was limited. Most of it was either at night or on your own. There was a lot of dart throwing, a lot of card games. It was the least business-like place I worked." As an art director who once worked with Della Femina says, "Before I met him I thought he was all smoke and mirrors. But at least then I thought it was real smoke and real mirrors." It's a quote that Jerry still finds hilarious.

He's very proud of the atmosphere. "We work very late," he said at the time. "We work until one, two in the morning every night almost. We start very early, we spend a lot of time together and we like each other. It's a nice feeling. There's music going on in the agency almost all the time. People are enjoying themselves, there's a lot of fun."

There was also a lot of boozing, marijuana, and sex. Jerry says, "We had a cleaning lady, Virginia, who swore when she wrote her book she'd make more money than anyone else. Because she caught every couple."

He expresses regret at the passing of their lascivious annual event, the agency Sex Contest. He claims it started when they first opened, and lasted for as long as thirty years:

"Everyone voted for the person they most wanted to go to bed with. There was a gay vote and *ménage-a-trois* vote, too. It was solemn vote counting, with poll watchers and everything. Talk about a well-kept secret; if it had come out, it would have destroyed us. It was the wildest thing, and good sophomoric fun. We'd do it around Christmas season. The winning couple would win a weekend at the Plaza Hotel. We don't know if anyone ever used it. I can't remember the second prize, but third place was offering Ron Travisano's couch. There were people who campaigned. One woman, an account person, had posters: 'Like Bloomingdale's, I'm open after 9 every night.'"

One year a prospective client, known to be a devout churchgoer, made a surprise visit to the agency a few days before the vote. Staff were rushing round the agency tearing down the more lewd posters as he was coming up in the elevator. They thought they'd got them all until he asked for the men's room. It was then that someone remembered one of the female staff had stuck little signs just above the urinal bowls: "Want any help with that? Vote for me!" They managed to keep him engaged in small talk just long enough to get the signs removed.

At the bottom of the voting paper there was always the slogan "Don't vote with your mind, vote with your loins." One year the vote count was overseen by the sober-suited and straight-faced agency auditors who happened to be in the offices that week.

"No one ever knew who'd voted for whom or even what the count was—all we ever announced was the result. It was all good unclean fun," Jerry recalls.

Bob Giraldi, the creative director who succeeded Bob Kuperman (and later moved on to direct Michael Jackson's "Beat it" video) has said he never even knew it took place. Told of this today, Jerry says, "What?" He calls to a man passing in the corridor, "Neil, Neil, Giraldi says he never knew about the sex parties."

A sleepy smile behind long grey hair. This is Neil Drossman, a veteran copywriter of those times. A dreamy gleam shines briefly in his eyes. "He won it one year."

"Yeah," confirms Jerry. "That's right. Why would he say that? He won it one year."

Who to believe? Memories twist and fade, the events themselves contorting the remembrance. They were days of laughter, of hedonism, of sensual indulgence: lotus-eating days.

AS THE QUALITY of the creative work began to gain recognition and importance within the business, so did the status and prestige of the creative people. This trend was accelerated in 1964 by a small blonde tornado who whirled into their world with an idea and a modus operandi that was as unique as anything they were doing—and just as lucrative.

Judy Wald had been a photographer's rep, employed to drum up commissions around town based on the quality of the work in the folio, her sassy attitude, and a forthright approach to potential customers. She had access to the senior creative people that a lot of young creative hopefuls were desperate to contact, but could reach only via a letter to their assistants at best. She realized she could be a bridge between the two, and was in pole position to start a creative employment agency.

Perhaps her cleverest move, very early on, was her radical fee structure. Normally set between 5 percent and 10 percent of the joining salary, this fee had always been paid by the employee, so the employing company considered, probably rightly, that they held all the cards. But Wald saw two steps ahead of this. If she got the companies to pay, the creative talent would flock to her for her free service. What would they have to lose? And if they flocked to her, then the companies seeking talent would naturally have to deal with her.

Wald opened her agency early in 1964, but she was not an immediate success. She had no trouble getting creative people on her books but the agencies didn't want to pay. For nearly a year she held out, valiantly refusing to cave in, but slowly beginning to believe it just wasn't going to work. Then the agency she least expected decided to play it her way.

She got a call from Leon Meadows, the creative department manager at DDB, giving her an employment brief and agreeing to pay the commission. She nearly fell off her chair.

ABOVE *Judy Wald in her office in the late 1960s .*

"I was speechless. I said to him, 'I don't want to do myself out of a job—but why you? People are clambering over each other to get in there!'"

But that was the problem for DDB—folios from hopeful art directors and writers were backing up down the corridors. Said Meadows, "I've just come from a meeting where we decided it was probably cheaper to pay your fees than use our time to sift through the books."

Wald couldn't have had a better start and she knew it. With the patronage of DDB, her fame and credibility on both sides of the industry rocketed, and she exploited both ceaselessly. She was a brilliant self-publicist, with the thick skin of a rhino and the chutzpah of her entrepreneurial Russian-Jewish immigrant grandfather. The fact that she was stylish, cute, almost gamine, with a sometimes biting dry wit didn't do her any harm in this wisecracking, fast-thinking, predominantly male environment.

She appeared all over Madison Avenue, at parties, dinners, executive lunches, and more parties. And if she didn't have an influential party to go to in the near future, she'd throw one. Before long, her opinions on creative work got her invited onto awards juries, a rare privilege for someone who didn't actually work in an agency, let alone a creative department. There was no one in the business who didn't know her, or of her, and she was indefatigable. Jerry Della Femina once got a call from her at 1:30 AM: "Being Italian, I feared the worst—a call in the middle of the night can only mean family trouble. But it was Judy—and all she said was, 'Jerry, I can't talk now' and hung up."

Wald was so embedded in the industry that Della Femina's agency featured her in a full page ad in an advertising trade magazine, *Advertising News of New York*, for Tio Pepe sherry. Written by Frank Giacomo, the copy took the form of a phone call to Wald asking her if she would do the endorsement.

For her reputation to be considered sufficiently influential to endorse a branded aperitif to the advertising elite was yet another step up for Wald. But read the copy and there's a slightly darker significance. Like an estate agent trying to sell a property she hasn't even seen, throughout the call she misunderstands Tio Pepe as the name of a new young foreign creative person. The role she plays is one of utter cynicism, careless of Pepe's talent or experience, she is simply trying to maximize his potential salary in his next job—and, naturally, her fee along with it. Pointing this out to her more than forty years later, she shrugs and laughs; "It was all a bit of fun. I was a controversial character." But the joke wasn't appreciated right across the business. In a July 1968 profile in *New York* magazine, written by a highly respected journalist Julie Baumgold (again a serious accolade for Judy), not everyone was unreservedly flattering.

"She's a people farmer," says one of Judy's golden boys. "She looks at a big agency like a field of wheat. Sometimes she stands looking up at an agency thinking, 'Here's a ripe copywriter, polish him up a little and send him over to Wells Rich Greene.' She can sell her harvest, the $15,000–$20,000 guy who moves a lot, again and again. In this business you hate to be on the bad side of Judy Wald if you're out of a job. She's the headhunter and you're the head."

When she offered exclusive contracts to agencies in return for an undertaking not to poach their staff (a move interpreted by many as only slightly short of protectionism), she further irritated the business. At Carl Ally Inc., Jim Durfee banned her from the premises.

But it bothered her little. Judy set up offices in Los Angeles, Chicago, London, Paris, Milan, and Dusseldorf and soon became the dominant force in creative recruitment in all those places as well—again, not always without annoying the locals. A British commercials company owner, who had helped her set up in London, banned her from his parties at Cannes. She had threatened to ruin his business in New York because he had helped a young creative person in London get a job for free. Judy felt that London was now her territory and told him so, in typically blunt New York terms.

Wald and the creative people were in a definite symbiosis and, despite the rumor and disapprobation swirling around her diminutive blonde head, her success was ongoing. It was a further indication of the growing importance of creative people.

IT WAS NOTHING LIKE AS EXCITING for the African-Americans. When Roger Sterling says to Don Draper, "BBDO have just employed their first negro—what do you think of that?," Don Draper replies sardonically, "I think I wouldn't want to be that negro."

Doug Alligood was that negro and forty-nine years later he's still at BBDO. He wasn't the first—Clarence Holte had been employed in 1952 in their "special markets" unit—but he was the next. And few have been employed since.

He was born in St. Louis in 1934. His father was a private handyman in rich homes, and would bring home discarded copies of magazines like *Saturday Evening Post* and *Life*, publications that no black child would normally have seen back then. Doug couldn't understand why there were no black people portrayed in the advertising other than stereotypes like Aunt Jemima and the I.W. Harper whisky waiter. "I wanted people in advertising who look like MY family—I had a couple of aunts who are nice-looking women, my mother was a nice-looking woman, my father was a good-looking guy, sure he was a handyman but so what? And I decided I wanted to get involved to change that."

Prevented from going to the whites-only Washington University in St. Louis, he studied Art at Bradley University in Peoria, Illinois (where he was barred from the Western Tap, the student hangout), and started work in a black-owned Detroit agency in 1956. After time in Korea he joined WCHB, a black-owned radio station, doing a little bit of everything— merchandising director, salesman, on the air. One of his clients was Bob Anderson, a BBDO executive working on the Pepsi business. He took a shine to Alligood and offered him a job as an account executive.

Whether he was enlightened or just appreciated which way the wind was blowing, Anderson was a great boss for the young Alligood. The Friday before he started, Anderson got the executives together and told them, "On Monday there will be a negro starting at BBDO. Now I don't want anybody to go out of their way to be good or bad, I want everybody to give the guy a fair shake. And by the way, if anybody can't abide by what I just said please step down to my office and we'll discuss your severance. And I mean *anybody*!"

Alligood was aware he had to be better than everyone else just to stand still, and although he was granted no favors nor leeway, he considers that he was never singled out or poorly treated. But he was lonely. As he says of the offices of Sterling Cooper, "Let off a shotgun around there and you're not going to hurt any black people!" He remembers playing in an agency softball league in a Detroit park one evening and seeing another African-American in the JWT team. "We embraced like we were long-lost brothers: 'I sure am glad to see you!'"

In 1964, he was transferred to New York. Since then, to his knowledge his color has been little handicap to any activity or work opportunity. If anything, his teetotal status was as much a barrier to a social life within the agency as the color of his skin.

His position in the company was not without its comic moments. Watching the expressions of space or time sales reps as they realized that the cultured Mr Alligood, with whom they'd made their appointment on the phone, was black was always entertaining. On another occasion the elevator in which he was traveling with an account executive of similar age and status stopped at the management floor. Just outside in the lobby was Charlie Brower, Chairman of BBDO, deep in conversation with another top executive. "Hi Doug," they both said before returning to their huddle. Doug waved casually, "Hi Charlie." The doors closed and the account man was awestruck. "They knew you, they knew your name, they knew you!"

"No big deal," said Alligood, "they've got hundreds of you—they only got one of me."

THAT THERE WERE SO FEW other blacks in the business was partly due to a lack of applicants. According to Stephen Forster in *The Mirror Makers*, David McCall at O&M interviewed hopeful copywriters every day for five years, and in that period he saw just three African-Americans. Black agencies existed, servicing clients aimed at the black market, but beyond that a job in an advertising agency just wasn't something the average black kid thought was available to them, janitor or elevator operator aside. As Alligood had seen in the white magazines, the world portrayed by advertising, based as it was on a white style and white imagery, seemed irrelevant, other-worldly.

There was plenty of agitation, and not just from outside the business, to get more black people into advertisements. Statistics were even published showing which agencies had employed how many black actors in their commercials—5 percent of all ads by 1967. Within a few years, some agencies had at least one African-American executive, but here Alligood suspected a rather sinister practice. He is convinced the agencies had a pact that whilst poaching of each other's staff was regular and accepted, that same poaching would not extend to black staff. Nobody wanted them to get above their station. By August 1967, a New York Commission on Human Rights survey of 40 agencies found only 3.5 of their staff were black—and the majority of those were in the lower paid jobs.

Despite its glossy image and apparent location at the cutting edge of style, advertising never really leads. It can only reflect back to society what society has already decided to do. It can't afford to set trends because if no one follows, it fails. It is subordinate to the state of the market and the whim of its clients. The severely limited spending power of black people— the 1960 US census showed median family annual income for whites to be $6,138, while the figure for nonwhites was just $3,351—made them largely irrelevant as targets for advertising.

As to the clients' whim, some of them in the sixties were still specifying "no Jews" on their business, let alone blacks, and it was a courageous agency that defied those client stipulations. By 1964, with the signing of the Civil Rights Act, the African-American was making progress in Washington but, despite the fact that the prevailing political posture of the new young creative people was liberal and Democratic, not on Madison Avenue.

IN THE MEANTIME Madison Avenue, was making progress of its own in Washington, or at least with the political parties there. The interest in DDB that had been expressed by Kennedy had been passed on to Johnson, and the agency was hired by the Democratic National Committee for his 1964 re-election campaign. Sid Myers and Stan Lee were assigned to the business.

Lee, the copywriter, was delighted. "I was very anti-Goldwater. I was also doing the advertising for a dog food at that time. Dog food, I had found out, doesn't excite me. But I could very easily get excited about beating Goldwater."

Their commercial, "Daisy," was electrifying. They showed an innocent little girl picking the petals off a daisy in a field of flowers. As she slowly counts them, a male voice, echoing from a PA, takes over. It becomes a sinister countdown. We slowly zoom into the girl's eyes as she looks up anxiously. As the countdown hits zero, the screen goes to a searing white, which we see is an expanding nuclear fireball. Johnson's voice says:

ABOVE *The "Daisy" advertisement, the prototype political TV commercial, created for Johnson's presidential campaign and aired only once, on September 7, 1964.*

VOTE FOR PRESIDENT JOHNSON ON NOVEMBER 3.

"These are the stakes. To make a world in which all God's children can live. Or go into the dark. We must either love each other or we must die." And then another male voice-over: "Vote for President Johnson on November third. The stakes are too high for you to stay home."

It's a remarkably moving thirty seconds. Watching it, you do feel involved and you don't want her to die. It's a reflex reaction to a simple visceral appeal. It clearly rattled the chairman of the Republican National Committee because he complained about it to his Democrat opponent in a news conference and got it taken off the air.

Lee takes up the story: "This immediately made what might have gone unseen, nationally famous. The commercial had run at the end of a very long, dull movie and not too many people had seen it. . . . And it appeared that night on the six o'clock news program as a news item. I could not have been happier."

It's the forerunner of much contemporary political advertising, featuring no politician, no policy statement, no statistics or happy citizens—simply a bold idea that insidiously casts the opponent as the bad guy and your man as the good guy, just by innuendo and without a single accusation.

It's also the forerunner of a technique much used since, particularly in political advertising: the ad as media event. You see a variation every year in the commercials in the half-time breaks at the Superbowl—make a controversial, expensive, or celebrity-soaked extravaganza and wait for the media to pick up on it and give you millions of dollars of free publicity.

One odd postscript to this campaign came after the release of papers in connection with the Watergate investigation, which included Nixon's somewhat paranoid "Most wanted list." Number four out of more than eight hundred names was the quiet and unassuming Mac Dane, down on the list as the representative of the agency that had done such devastating work for the Democrats. Why Doyle and Bernbach escaped the honor is not recorded.

CONTROVERSY—SHOCK EVEN—rapidly became the handmaiden of advertising, often misused and misplaced. But throughout the 1960s, on one specific project, George Lois used shocking impact time and again with pinpoint accuracy.

In September 1962, just before the Liston-Patterson World Heavyweight title fight, an edition of *Esquire* magazine had appeared on the bookstands with a photograph of a boxer who looked identical to Floyd Patterson, spread-eagled on the canvas under the lights of a totally deserted auditorium. The line under the masthead read, "Last man in the ring. Sonny Liston and Floyd Patterson talk about being tough and scared."

This was the first of nearly a hundred *Esquire* covers that Lois conceived and designed in a run stretching until 1972. It was highly risky for several reasons: first, it was unlike most magazine covers because it distilled the contents down to just one lead story; second, the execution was pointed and controversial. Liston had a conviction for armed robbery, suspected mob connections, and was in constant trouble with the police. So unsavory was his image that the National Association for the Advancement of Colored People (NAACP) urged Patterson not to fight for fear of the backlash a Liston win might bring; third, in portraying not so much a Liston win as a Patterson defeat, Lois was sticking his neck out against a number of fight pundits who were calling a Patterson victory.

He would be first to admit that if he was taking a risk, it was nothing compared to that taken by his client, Managing Editor Harold Hayes. "He was a gem," says Carl Fischer, the photographer Lois used on the overwhelming majority of executions. "He was a southern gentleman. He wanted to do great work at *Esquire*. They didn't have a lot of money but he managed to entice a lot of people to work for him. Because he would give them their head, ask for their opinions."

Hayes did everything a good client of any creative endeavor should do: he shortened the lines of communication and approval (to just him), simplified the briefing and, having chosen Lois, backed his ideas. Time and again he went out on a limb for controversial concepts. He was rewarded with a 400 percent sales increase over the ten years. Not all of that can be attributed to the covers, but there can be no doubt that they helped enormously.

Hayes approached Lois in the summer of 1962 simply for advice on how better to present the magazine. The more Lois got into the convoluted and byzantine ways in which a committee of people would decide what went on the cover and then stumble to the approval of whatever ideas were presented ("group grope" as Lois contemptuously dismisses it), the itchier he became to get involved. It wasn't a job for PKL and Lois didn't approve of freelance, but he offered to do a couple of covers on spec.

Although not strictly an advertising project, Lois's idea was to approach it as such. Demonstrating the difference between a designer and an advertising art director, he went beyond simply laying out graphic elements in an eye-catching fashion, making the cover a narrative idea. "It helps to sell the magazine. If you do a cover correctly, . . . it almost crystallizes what the magazines want to say. And in fact there have been times when I've done covers that have crystallized that point, with a change of direction inside."

Other than the photograph and a short pithy line, there was nothing on the front apart from the date and *Esquire* masthead. Not only did this help the magazine stand out against the visual tumult of the news stands, but their domination on the page enhanced the explosive nature of the ideas.

THE COVERS WERE frequently controversial. With the quietly set line "The Passion of Muhammad Ali," one showed Ali in boxing gear pierced by arrows, in the style of St. Sebastian. Another featured a Norman Rockwell-esque child, complete with coke and hamburger, looking in shock at a TV set showing Jack Ruby killing Lee Oswald. Although the story is about the background to the killing, the picture takes it onto a further plane, the loss of American innocence.

On another cover, Andy Warhol falls backward into a can of Campbell's tomato soup to signify the end of pop art. Warhol was excited; he thought they were going to make a giant can and fill it with soup. Fischer shot the picture in two parts, dropping a marble into a can of thinned soup to make the splash and then stripping in a separate shot of Warhol.

As Fischer remembers it, "We had a green room where we stuck people with pastries while they were waiting for the [shoot]. My daughter who was maybe ten at the time went down there and saw Warhol and he said. 'I'm bored, I'm bored', and she said, 'I just got a homework assignment—let me bring it down'. It was a map of the United States and she was supposed to color it in—and Andy Warhol colored it in for her. She didn't know who he was. But he didn't go over the lines. She was very happy with it".

"Creativity can solve almost any problem. The creative act, the defeat of habit by originality, overcomes everything."

GEORGE LOIS

Fischer and Lois worked well together. At the time Lois said of Fischer, "He understands what I'm trying to do. I explain the ad and I don't explain the picture. He understands the advertising. He's a good art director himself. I'd rather talk to Carl than talk to a technician because he understands it all."

Yet another controversial cover showed Nixon's face, beset by four hands holding makeup, including lipstick, to the caption, "Nixon's last chance— this time he'd better look right." It's a reference to the terrible impression he made on the TV debates against Kennedy in 1960, pale, sweating, with a heavy jowl shadow, that supposedly cost him the election. Lois says he got a phone call from an incensed White House aide: "We know what you're trying to do. You're trying to make him look like a faggot!"

ONE OF LOIS' FAVORITE covers, and one of the most ambiguous images imaginable, was taken by Fischer for the November 1970 issue. On March 16, 1968, between 350 and 500 Vietnamese (mainly women and children, some of whom had been sexually abused and tortured) were massacred in the hamlets of My Lai and My Khe by a unit of the US Army under the command of Lieutenant "Rusty" Calley. Just before Calley's trial, *Esquire* decided to publish extracts from a book about him and this became the subject for the cover.

Fischer's photograph shows a seated Calley, surrounded by trusting Asian children, smiling broadly like an indulgent older brother. It was shot in Fischer's East Eighty-third Street studio.

"It was very straightforward to do." He thinks for a moment. "One of the things that amazes me is why people let their pictures be taken in such compromising situations. . . . I had observed in all the years of working

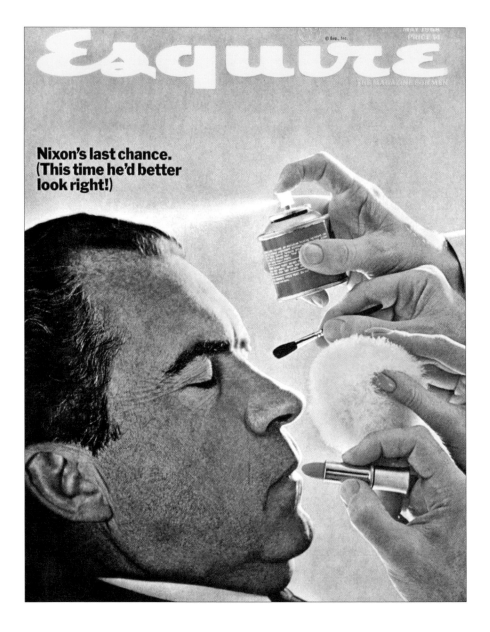

ABOVE AND OPPOSITE *A selection of the most scintillating and shocking* Esquire *covers created by George Lois in the 1960s.*

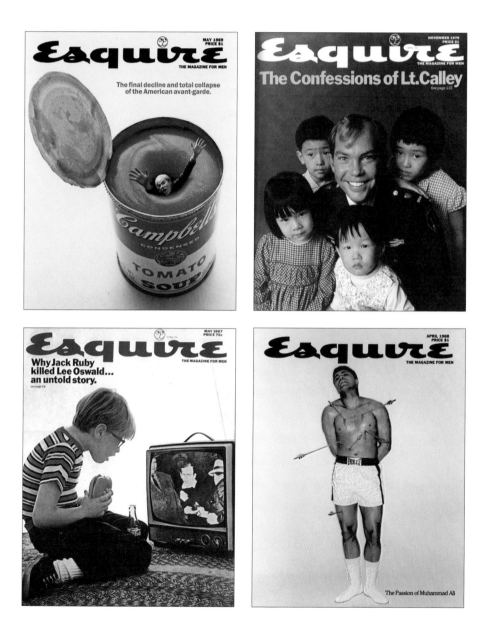

only one or two people ever refuse to do something on the cover on the magazine. It's important promotion for people. . . . I mean, did he understand what was happening? I mean, how stupid can you be?"

When asked if Calley may have thought it was expiation, Fischer says, "I really don't know what he thought. Expiation would be the last thing I would think of. I think he would think, 'Look, I'm friendly with kids', but who knows what he thought? The fact that he did it at all was extraordinary."

He parodies Lois' brief: 'This fucking fuck is going to sit around these fucking kids and we're going to take a crazy picture."

Lois had him pose unsmiling and then smiling, and decided the smiling one was the one he wanted. He is ambiguous even about its ambiguity. "It meant different things to different people. A lot of people who thought the war was terrific looked at it and said 'Calley, he said he didn't do anything wrong. Maybe he killed . . . but he fought for this country, he doesn't look guilty.' Other people looked at it and were shocked, saying, 'That son of a bitch, killer, sitting there with children he killed.'"

It was the most controversial from a decade of controversial covers. It offended a lot of people. Lois isn't bothered. He bathes in the reaction and exults in the uproar.

9 Thinking Big

"We're being bought by McCann— do you know what that means?"

DON DRAPER TO PEGGY OLSEN **MAD MEN**

In a triumphalist piece in *New York* magazine Jerry Della Femina proclaimed the old-style agencies vanquished by the creative revolutionaries who were now carousing uninhibitedly up and down the Avenue. It actually appeared in the April 27, 1970, edition but one section could have been published at any time from the early sixties, with increasing accuracy as the decade went on.

"In a sense [clients of] the older agencies are asking for divorces, and then they're running out with these young chicks. And so what the older agencies do is try to act like a woman who is trying to hold onto her husband. . . . The older agencies go out and buy a load of cosmetics and eyeshadow and they put all this stuff on and do their hair—this is what they're doing when they start hiring freaky young kids at star salaries." Della Femina should know—he'd only recently been the happy recipient of a handsome salary from Bates for exactly that reason.

The older agencies were fairly certain they knew what their clients wanted—more of what they'd been giving them for years. But even in the late fifties as Benton & Bowles demonstrated when they hired newer, edgier creative people like Amil Gargano and Ed McCabe, they were already looking over their shoulders at this strange new competition coming up on them. As the decade went on they thought they should have a few more exotic writers and art directors around to prevent their clients from flirting with the newer, sexier agencies.

JWT, still the largest agency, took it one stage further when in 1967 they lured Ron Rosenfeld away from DDB to be their creative director on a record $100,000 salary. It was a Judy Wald placement and widely recognized as a gamble; Lore Parker, still happily at DDB, said at the time, "It never seems to work for an old-line conservative agency to bring in DDB people to work under the old system. I am holding my breath to see what will happen with Ron Rosenfeld going to JWT." She didn't have to hold it for long. You can't graft one culture onto another—unless there's a massive upheaval, the existing culture will always squeeze out the interloper. Within eighteen months the experiment was over and Rosenfeld had left to set up his own agency with Len Sirowitz and Marion Harper—Harper, Rosenfeld, and Sirowitz.

BY MID-DECADE the gulf between Old and New had become a chasm. Bernbach's style of advertising and of running an agency was either loved or loathed—there was no halfway point. Shorthanded as "Creative Advertising," it was either the curse or the savior of the industry.

Driven by a combination of incomprehension and fear—and some justifiable concern as much of the new work was not conceived with the discipline of DDB's creative department—the criticism came from those agencies too inert, and with clients too entrenched, to adapt.

Barton Cummings, President of Compton-Advertising, the major P&G agency responsible for some of the dreariest of Madison Avenue's output, described it in Richard Gilbert's *Marching up Madison Avenue* as as "The Museum of Modern Art School of Advertising" and accused it of wasting clients' money. "What really produces sales is not art work but solid merchandising, research, and media spadework backed by straightforward, convincing advertising." You can hear the quivering indignation.

The creative side, when it could be bothered, hit back. In a brilliant satire, *Communication Arts* magazine gravely demonstrated the "shortcomings" of DDB's "Think Small" (see overleaf) and step by step systematically ruined it by showing how a Compton style agency would have "improved" the ad. It attracted at least one approving letter.

Nine Ways to Improve an Ad

Rule: Show the product.

Don't turn it into a postage stamp or a test of failing eyesight. Show it. Boldly. Dramatically. Excitingly. Like this:

Think small.

There. See the difference already? Now, I'll admit the headline no longer makes complete sense—but that brings us to another obvious improvement.

Rule: Don't use negative headlines.

"Think Small" may be very clever, very witty...but what an idea to leave in the minds of everyday readers.

Think **BIG!**

"Think BIG!" Now I ask you—isn't that better? Isn't it more positive, more direct? And note, too, the interesting use of type to punch home the excitement of the idea.

Well that brings us to still another improvement—and one of the most important rules in advertising.

Rule: Whenever possible, mention your product name in the headline.

Which the people who thought up this ad could have done so very, very easily.

Think **BIG** and you'll choose **VOLKSWAGEN!**

See how the ad is beginning to jell? How it's really starting to come alive.

Let's see another way we can breathe some life into it—with a warming touch of humanity.

Rule: Whenever possible, show people enjoying your product.

Think *BIG* and you'll choose *Volkswagen*

That's more like it. A gracious mansion. A carefree band of dancers. And best of all, a proud pair of thoroughbreds.

Now for an improvement to correct a fault in the product itself. You'll note that the VW, unfortunately, is totally lacking in news. From year to year, while other cars bring out a host of exciting changes—it stays its own dowdy self.

Rule: Always feature news in your advertisement. And if you have no news, invent it. Like this:

New from Volkswagen! A '63 sizzler with new sass and skeedaddle!

How's that for news?

Rule: (One of the most obvious of the bunch) **Always give prominent display to your product logo.**

And I don't mean an arty jumble of initials no one can read; I mean a proud unashamed logo like this:

New from Volkswagen! A '63 sizzler with new sass and skeedaddle!

There. Now they know who's paying for the ad!

Rule: Avoid all unpleasant connotation about your product.

Which brings us to a somewhat delicate area: the country of origin of the Volkswagen car. Now I don't have to dwell on the subject of World War II and its attendant unpleasantness for you to grasp my meaning. Let's simply say that it might be wise to "domesticate" the car, so to speak.

VOLKSWAGEN—THE ALL-AMERICAN CAR!

And in a flash, apple strudel turns into good old apple pie!

Rule: Always tell the reader where he can buy your product.

Where can you buy a Volkswagen?

"At your friendly authorized Volkswagen dealer." Note the warmth of words like "friendly." And the use of "Authorized" to make sure that prospects don't stumble into places that are unauthorized.

One rule to go. The most important rule of all.

Rule: Always localize your ads.

And mind the way you spell the dealer's names.

There you have it. No clever, precious, self-conscious waste of space like the ad we started with; but an honest hard-hitting, two-fisted ad like this that really sells.

I said "sells." ∎

In business terms the "creative" agencies and the clients they represented were a tiny proportion of total advertising activity. Nevertheless, the noise within the trade was coming entirely from them. In 1965 when Mobil, at the time a major gasoline advertiser, took their business from Bates and gave it to DDB, it was perceived if not as the beginning of the end, at least the end of the beginning of the Creative Revolution, with the spoils going to the renegades.

At Bates, Reeves suddenly retired, claiming it had always been his intention to go at fifty-five. There's some evidence to suggest that he was beginning to wonder whether he'd got it all entirely right after all. He confided to Ed McCabe that he felt "over positioned," that he'd found himself, as a necessary business gambit, defending the tasteless work he'd secretly begun to hate.

Ogilvy & Mather (they'd dropped the Benson in 1964) was growing healthily but the agency's reputation for interesting and original work was a fast-fading memory, stuck as they were with Ogilvy's rigid and increasingly discredited rules.

BUT BIG WASN'T NECESSARILY all bad. Y&R had maintained a degree of creative integrity for several decades and flourished in the new atmosphere. They found the perfect creative leader for their times in Steve Frankfurt, an intelligent and articulate art director. Yet another student of Alexey Brodovitch and the Pratt Institute, Frankfurt's initial experience had been in film, and he brought that to bear in his advertising career, approaching commercials in a less rigid way than had hitherto been attempted.

Most commercials shot by New York agencies in the fifties and early sixties were made by three major companies, with technicians and directors more used to shooting live commercials within sponsored programs. Many had limited experience of the wider aspects of filmmaking yet they controlled the business, treating the process like a factory production line, exercising minimum imagination and very little effort, while the creative teams were given almost no role in the execution of their ideas.

The revolutionizing of this system aided the larger Creative Revolution. Photographers who had previously been employed by agencies for stills shoots gradually began to be used by those same agencies for commercials. They brought a few advantages: they had already worked in color and were ready for its increasing presence in TV commercials throughout the sixties; they were used to the ways of the advertising system and understood the relationship between creative people and the account people, the agency and the client; and they were more prepared to cooperate.

At Carl Ally, Amil Gargano found the director that their agency producer had hired to shoot their first Volvo commercials patronizing, inflexible, and lacking in enthusiasm. He fired him after the first day and employed Mike Cuesta, a photographer he'd used before. It was the start of Cuesta's career as a commercials director.

Irving Penn, Steve Horn, Bert Stern, and Harold Becker all trod the same path, while Bob Giraldi and George Gomes made the switch across from agency art director. Howard Zeiff, who'd shot stills for Levy's and Polaroid for DDB in the fifties, became the most awarded and sought-after director of the late sixties. His reel by 1970 was a roll call of the absolute best of US advertising, stories told with exquisite timing and bathed in humanity; affectionate, realistic and always funny.

As an art director at Y&R, Frankfurt saw his commercials with an imaginative advertiser's eye, asking for techniques and ideas that wouldn't have occurred to the hidebound directors who were normally employed. A spot with no words at all was unheard of then but it didn't stop Frankfurt; for Johnson & Johnson he shot a baby in close-up from the mother's point of view rather than the conventional posed setup, making it more personal and emotional. He used stop-motion and borrowed from contemporary art—he saw no barriers to where you could go to make a commercial.

His talent and creative leadership skills earned him the presidency of the agency in 1967, unprecedented for an art director. Of all the agencies that predated DDB, Y&R under Frankfurt's leadership was the only one to garner any respect from the new creative generation, with such work as their emotional Wings of Man campaign for Eastern Airlines. But in 1971, at the age of forty, he stepped down, later saying, "I never had a frustrating day in that company—until I became president."

He went back to Hollywood to a new career in film publicity, back to his core skill as an art director. Amongst his subsequent output was the world-famous poster for *Rosemary's Baby*.

Back on Madison Avenue, according to a *Newsweek* article on the state of US advertising, in the first seven months of 1969 more than a hundred new agencies had started up. This is a little difficult to believe—that's roughly two every three working days—but it does reflect the optimistic fervor with which the creative community regarded the business. As the article says, "Most of them have been the undertaking of one to four young creative people who have served a term with an old-line agency . . . who seek . . . the freedom to exercise their talents (and dress) as they wish."

Their dress, in keeping with the times, had transformed since the day those sixteen Italian art directors lined up for their shoot. *Newsweek* reported the head of one of the leading agencies as saying, "You should see the things walking around back in our creative department. Frazzled hair, denims, neckerchiefs, the works." Another said, "My God! We hired a new copywriter the other day—a very good one—and he came to work in his bare feet!" Fifteen years earlier Al Reis, a young account man at a Madison Avenue industrial agency, received a querulous all-staff memo from the president demanding that male staff wear knee-length socks so that no bare leg would show when they sat down.

Enthusiasm is one thing, foresight is another. Already there were signs that perhaps this "freedom to exercise their talents" was not all it appeared to be. PKL had already imploded, the partners barely speaking to each other. Koenig, by his own admission, was bored and absent a lot of the time, Lois was angry, and Papert was distracted by the demands of running what was now a public company. By 1967, Lois had left with Ron Holland to set up Lois Holland Callaway.

Further, the move to gain respectability and transparency by going public had apparently backfired; according to Papert, far from making the agency look respectable "PKL looked like it was doing better than P&G. They accused us of looking after ourselves rather than P&G."

BUT NONE OF THIS turbulence had any effect on the one man whose ideas were light years away from the writers and art directors cavorting in their newfound freedoms. Marion Harper Jr. had set his sights on issues, both personal and professional, of truly immense consequence.

This is the diver of Acapulco. Some men say he is crazy, but he is not. He just likes to dive. He stands on the edge of a hundred and sixty foot-high cliff and throws himself into nine feet of water. He does this eleven times each day. But Acapulco is like that. A little mad. A little wild. Starting July 1st Eastern begins the first non-stop jet service to Acapulco. You can fly there from Kennedy at 6:55 p.m. Wednesdays and Fridays. Or you can fly via Mexico City on Monday, Thursday and Saturday. Make this the summer you see Acapulco. A whole, wonderful week of it. And pay us later with Eastern's new Charge-A-Trip plan. It only costs about $17 a month complete with air fare. Ask your Travel Agent. Or talk to us at 661-3000 or at 621-9450 in New Jersey. Once you see the diver of Acapulco, you will never forget him. You will never forget Acapulco.

EASTERN

ABOVE *A campaign for Eastern Airlines, "The Wings of Man," created by Steve Frankfurt at Young & Rubicam. This advertisement was on the author's office wall in London in the late 1960s.*

Harper joined McCann-Erickson, a large New York agency, in 1939 at the age of twenty-three as a trainee. Nine years later he was the president. That his trajectory through the ranks of what was a very conservative company was so rapid came as no surprise to those who knew of his phenomenal work ethic, focus, and intellect.

Born in Oklahoma in 1916, his precocity was quickly obvious. At the age of ten he was addressing the United Daughters of the Confederacy in the Oklahoma State Capitol on his chosen subject, "The Time is Here for the North and South to Forget their Differences and Pull Together." His mother, an occasional newspaper columnist who was both politically and socially aware, brought him up after his father, a newspaper space salesman, had left the family and moved to New York.

Harper worked diligently at school and after two years at Andover went to Yale, leaving in 1938 with top honors in math, economics, and psychology. His father, by then a vice president of General Foods, was an early believer in marketing and distribution research. It was a leaning that rubbed off on Marion; he'd worked his summer vacations as a door-to-door salesman, mainly of women's goods, experimenting on the relative effectiveness of different sales pitches.

The following year he started in the postroom at McCann Erickson at 285 Madison Avenue. Hanging around the research department and asking endless questions laced with a few ideas of his own quickly got him promoted, and he was given his own research project to oversee, a method of testing ad copy prior to publication. He was mind-numbingly diligent in his analysis and by the age of twenty-six he was head of copy research, by thirty director of research, and by thirty-two, in 1948, president of McCann-Erickson.

By now he was married, with two children, not that he saw much of them—the next decade was outstanding for McCann and there's no question that it was the result of Harper's indefatigable effort. From fifth place in terms of agency size, with billings of $50 million, the company had a period of growth matched only by BBDO; by 1959 McCann Erickson was second only to JWT in size, billing $231 million.

He was personally quiet, "actually shy, a lonesome man, the company was his life," says Carl Spielvogel, an executive who worked closely with him from 1960. But Harper's moves were bold and unconventional. In

1958, in an almost unprecedented act, he resigned the Chrysler account for the smaller Buick business, believing that being on the GM roster represented the better opportunity for his agency's growth. It wasn't a popular move, but Harper's judgement proved to be right.

He was careful, too, to nourish McCann's already advanced global reach. Again, it was only JWT that could better McCann's international client roster by 1960. One gain in particular was Coca-Cola, which became a flagship business for the agency. The agency won the account precisely because Coca Cola's incumbent agency, D'Arcy, had shown no great enthusiasm to offer the overseas services that Coca-Cola needed and subsequently found at the vigorously global McCann.

In the business of the industry, Harper always seems to have been several steps ahead of everyone else. "He was a brilliant conceptualist. He could formulate ideas that took the industry quite a while to catch up with" says Spielvogel. He had a fearsome intellect, a ferocious work ethic, frequently putting in twenty-four-hour stretches, and phenomenal concentration. He would regularly astonish colleagues in new business presentations by displaying a detailed knowledge of the minutiae of, say, the prospective client's regional market share or pricing policy, even though he'd been handed the fat briefing documents only two hours before the meeting.

TALL, BALD, AND HEAVY SET, this focus did not make Harper approachable, although it gained him respect; in a 1963 *Time* magazine article, an unnamed agency president said, "While I find Marion unattractively impersonal and ruthless, he does seem to be a marvelous organizer, and his mental capacity is immense."

His capacity for innovative thinking was unending. Most of it seemed to come from a mind obsessed with research, especially with finding out what made things work and then implementing improved versions of them. He also had the ability to rise way above the daily grind; whilst being super-diligent about detail he would also be first with what we now call a "helicopter view."

A lot of McCann's appeal to clients was based around new and seductive research tools, encouraged by Harper. They were attracted to techniques with reassuringly technical names, such as the Relative Sales Conviction

Test, which apparently guaranteed advertising success. How could you fail if your ads had been tested, for example, in The Perception Laboratory? This was a concept shown to him by a Dr. Eckhart Hess at the University of Chicago, which he adapted and modified to analyze responses to advertising by measuring the pupil dilation of interviewees while being shown various visual stimuli.

He was a seer; he is credited with being the first person to coin the term "think tank." He was the first to describe the wider function of an ad agency as "marketing communications." thirty years before the phrase became common usage. He arrived at the term partly because he was one of the first people to urge his staff to think beyond advertising on behalf of their clients. As early as 1960 he was talking about "holistic" answers to marketing problems (another industry buzzword thirty years later). He was enthusing about the coming "information explosion" and he had a prescient interest in computers. Many of these ideas came from the Institute of Communications Research, a McCann think tank to shape all the other think tanks, a department to improve the agency's primary functions.

One notion, typical of the extraordinary breadth of his imagination and his fascination for the concept of the group thinking—together with his talent for packaging his ideas—was best described by Russ Johnston in his book, *Marion Harper: An Unauthorized Biography*, a riveting account of this intriguing man and his unusual story:

"He called it 'The Humanivac' a combination obviously of 'Human' and 'Univac,' as the then most popular computer was known. His idea was to assemble people like parts of a giant brain, each specializing in a particular aspect of marketing. A problem would be presented, each part of the human machine would go into action, and in a short time the solution would roll out, neatly packaged and ready to go to market. Some people thought it was fortunate that the idea slowly disappeared. Today [1982] it seems feasible but in 1962 it seemed pretty far-fetched. But, then, so was putting a man on the moon."

His most obvious and publicly recognized goal was to overtake JWT in size. But a much later remark, talking about his aims at the time he was made president, reveals a much grander vision: "At thirty-eight . . . you can't have as your ambition just to be the best of whatever there already

ABOVE *Marion Harper; a brilliant mind—but flawed.*

is." He was always going to do something different and new and the idea that changed not just McCann Erickson but the entire business out of all recognition was so devastatingly simple it seems incredible that advertising could have got so far without anyone having thought of it before. He invented the advertising conglomerate.

THE IDEA WAS driven by clients' deep abhorrence of sharing their advertising agent with any other client who could be conceived as a rival, no matter how remote. They claim it's to preserve confidentiality, but the information passing through an advertising agency can rarely be more sensitive than that passing through auditors, corporate law firms, and banks—companies that rival clients are perfectly happy to share. Agencies comply because they have no choice but it means that none can ever handle more than one account in each category; one car, one toothpaste, one airline. (In *Mad Men* Sterling Cooper had to resign Mohawk Airlines to be free to pitch for American Airlines.)

So when one advertising agency acquired another, any conflict would have to be resolved, and usually this meant that the smaller of the conflicting accounts would be resigned. This immediately reduced the value of the merger, with two plus two often making no more than three.

Then Harper, in his words, "turned the management ladder sideways" and started a practice where the acquired agency would operate independently of the acquiring agency, but they would be financially bound by a holding company above them, the beneficiary of their joint profits. Ridiculously simple. But, amazingly, for advertising completely original.

There was a second dimension to the idea, one that has possibly had the greater reverberations through the business ever since. Harper figured that though agencies supplied clients with ancillary services like research, promotions advice and publicity, they never properly charged for them. Because they were located within the agency and were delivered largely by the same team who delivered their advertising, the client perception was that they weren't a separate service and there should not be a significant fee for them.

So his idea was that specialist companies—Marplan, specializing in market research, Communications Counselors Inc. for publicity, and Sales

Communications Inc. for sales promotions—should be set up to provide those services outside the agencies. Initially a number of their staff were actually the people who'd been doing those jobs within the agencies—no matter, their specific expertise and experience would be properly and separately charged for, and their profits would go to the holding company. Economies of scale would be achieved by having as much common back-room staff to service the agencies and specialist companies as possible—administration, purchasing, finance—located in the holding company.

The holding company therefore sat on top of a variety of independently operating and competing advertising agencies, each of which could cross-refer business to a variety of equally independent specialist support service companies. Extend this overseas, float it on the stockmarket and you have the prototype of the contemporary marketing services conglomerate like WPP or Omnicom.

Though Harper himself described what he was creating as a "revolution," it was far from the Creative Revolution over at DDB. Indeed, he had as great a suspicion of it as Bart Cummings, attacking in a major management meeting "the new cult of creativity . . . closely identified with the bizarre." He was poles apart from Bernbach, whose comment, "I warn you against believing advertising is a science" was in flat contradiction of everything Harper believed. He wasn't neglectful of the creative side but, typically, he viewed it as yet another area that would benefit from the analytical and think-tank-based approach—and he set up yet another Interpublic subsidiary company.

Spielvogel describes it as "a sort of combination of think tank and creative center. It was thinking out how the projects should go creatively, and then turning over the grunt work, the media and development of the creative work, to the agency. Harper called it 'co-creativity'—what happens when you blend different skills at a very high level. We're conducting an experiment to learn whether through co-creativity you can produce better, neater, brighter, hotter, more creatively."

It was to be called Jack Tinker & Partners, the partners element indicating that each of the four members (Jack Tinker, an art director; Dr. Herta Herzog, an Austrian psychologist expert in motivational research; Don Calhoun, a copywriter; and Myron McDonald, the marketing director) had an equal voice.

BORN IN PITTSBURGH, Tinker had made his way up through the ranks as an art director until the attack on Pearl Harbor in 1941. He tried to enlist, saying in a 1982 interview: "I sat there for two days in my underwear and eventually somebody examined me and I passed and the last question was 'Where did you go to college?', and I said, 'Well, I didn't go to college. I went to this art school.' As soon as I said that the noncommissioned officer, whoever he was, said, 'That's all. Put your pants on and get out.'"

Tinker went briefly to JWT but McCann got him back as creative director. In the latter years of the fifties he'd been somewhat sidelined—one curious feature of Harper's casting for Jack Tinker & Partners was that all four of the partners had been left out of the mainstream of agency operations.

The agency started off in the Waldorf Towers in 1964 but they didn't last long there—the comings and goings of clients, messenger boys, deliveries and all the noisy circus of office life alerted their classy neighbors—General Douglas MacArthur on the floor below, the Duke and Duchess of Windsor above. The terms of the lease forbidding use of the premises for business were enforced and they were out on their collective ear. They moved to a suite in the Dorset Hotel, previously owned by Martin Revson, the owner of Revlon cosmetics. They weren't exactly slumming it. Charlie Moss, a young writer who'd been hired by Tinker from DDB on more than double his previous salary, describes the scene:

"It was really a *Mad Men* set—the main room was two stories high with a kind of a balcony round the top, everything was white, the furniture was white with a white baby grand piano in the middle of the room. Around this big central conference room and living room place were other offices, which were hotel suites/rooms. When we came in they said they didn't have any more room on that floor, so they put us on a different floor. They gave us a suite of a living room and two bedrooms that were our office, no furniture, just a carpet. The first three weeks we did everything on the floor."

Who did what is not clear, but judged against Harper's initial brief there was some success. "The first piece of business we had was [from] the Bulova Watch Company . . . although when we got it, it was a piece of machinery that had been a spin off from the Space Program," recalls Jack Tinker. The agency helped Bulova decide how to use it, then designed and named it—The Accutron Watch—and helped them get it into shops like Abercrombie & Fitch, a very different sort of store from the A&F of today.

Next they helped with the design, naming, and styling of the Buick Riviera, followed by projects for Coca-Cola, Exxon, product design for Westinghouse, and providing input for Interpublic new business presentations. Then they took on a project for their first direct client, Miles Laboratories, and their success with it changed the nature of the organization completely.

The Alka Seltzer account had been won in comical circumstances; Miles didn't want it known that their account was loose, and Harper and his team had flown to their headquarters at Elkhart, Indiana, in his eccentric corporate aeroplane, a converted bomber. While the meeting was underway the plane was backed into fresh concrete at a dispersal area at the airport. Their attempt at discretion was blown as the local newspaper the next day ran the story of the Interpublic plane conspicuously sunk in cement.

The advertising idea could not have been simpler: as the male voice-over says, "No matter what shape your stomach's in . . . when it gets out of shape . . . take Alka Seltzer," and accompanying it we see a series of stomachs—flat, fat, and flabby—shown in close-up in everyday use: a road digger, a ballet dancer, a fat man having his stomach jabbed by another man with whom he is in urgent conversation, and a mechanic easing himself under a car. Under Howard Zieff's sympathetic direction the campaign was warm, affectionate and infectious, and the jaunty tune written by Sascha Burland, which reached number thirteen in the Billboard chart, helped delight the United States and revitalize Alka Seltzer.

The campaign was so unlike anything ever seen for a pharmaceutical product before. The follow-up was animated, a cartoon man berated by his stomach (played by Gene Wilder), complaining about the rich food he eats. The dialogue is fast and witty, like a Woody Allen exchange. And with the strap line "When you and your stomach don't agree" the viewer was again charmed by a commercial in a category in which they were more used to being bullied by Rosser Reeves' doctors in lab coats and crashing hammers in animated heads.

The industry acclaim for the campaign changed the perception of Jack Tinker & Partners from an experimental creative think tank to that of a full-fledged creative hot shop. Indeed, history now portrays Harper's motive as being much like those agencies that Della Femina lambasted in his article, setting it up as a satellite for more adventurous clients who may have thought of leaving the unadventurous McCann. But Harper came to regret letting Tinker take the business as their own client, rather than continuing to work on a project basis only: "I should have continued some immediate provision for experimental creative principles. Because what happened was that the client began to eat up the people."

In the same interview he credited Dr. Herzog (the model for Dr. Greta Guttman, the European research director at Sterling Cooper who enraged Draper with her recommendations for Lucky Strike advertising) with the simple suggestion that two rather than one Alka Seltzer tablets was required. The result? Double the sales!

TINKER WAS PROVING to be yet another successful addition to Harper's new and burgeoning group. The first acquisition had been Marschalk and Pratt in 1954, an agency with which McCann shared the Standard Oil—Exxon—business. Amongst others added to the mix over the coming years were the New York and London offices of Pritchard Wood, a British agency, and Erwin Wasey. Initially the agencies and ancillary companies were owned by McCann but operated entirely autonomously. The final move was to take the name of a public relations company McCann owned in Germany, Interpublic—easy to say, spell and understand in any country—and incorporate it as the holding company for Harper's empire in 1961. Flotation wasn't to happen for another ten years but meanwhile, all was going well for the "emperor"—except that increasingly his courtiers were beginning to wonder whether he was wearing any clothes.

"Marion was always more interested in the top line than the bottom line," says Spielvogel. Harper had employed him personally in 1960 from writing his daily advertising column for the *New York Times* as his executive assistant, specifically to work on the establishment of Interpublic. He did well, and by 1967 was vice president and on the main board of Interpublic, handling the Miller Beer account and responsible for new business acquisition and press relations.

Looking back, he says of Harper, "When he was building the company he was a brilliant business conceptualist and then he became enamored with growth at any price. And there was a big price to pay."

Harper's operating style, both professional and personal, was becoming increasingly grand and expansive. His emphasis on internal training and education for his staff in the latest techniques and procedures cost huge sums in the enormous and elaborate global meetings that he would stage. The chase for new business was relentless and he had no interest in keeping down the costs for pitches.

In less than four days in 1965, for a $10 million piece of GM business, he had fifty copies of a detailed presentation written and printed in full quality hard back book form. Says Russ Johnston, "The cost . . . must have been enormous. The craftsmen were union workers and the plate making, typesetting, printing and binding were done on a weekend overtime basis." Johnston estimates the cost of an equally unsuccessful pitch for TWA in 1967 at more than $200,000.

The balances that had kept him in check had fallen away; Harry McCann, the man who had employed and guided him in his early years, had long since retired and subsequently been killed in a car crash. And the long-term chief financial officer Burt Stilson, suffered a heart attack and retired to Florida to play golf.

"A lot of people who reach a certain point start to smell the roses," said one contemporary observer. Harper's personal life, too, was becoming stratospherically high octane. Bizarrely, he invested heavily and unwisely in prize cattle, and for his second wife, Valerie Feit ("long legged, radiant, beautiful," according to Russ Johnston), he set up a fashion consultancy in Paris under the Interpublic banner. It was a loss maker.

His most public vice was the acquisition of corporate aircraft, ridiculed across Madison Avenue as Harper's Airforce. He capped them all in 1965 with the purchase of a DC7 from KLM. Seating more than 150 people, it was as pointless an acquisition as it was expensive. After several months of conversion, it emerged with a state-of-the-art office and a drawing room with brass standard lamps, gold deep-pile rugs, a sumptuous sofa in glove leather, Eames chairs and silk wall coverings. The bedroom had a full-size bed and tiled shower, while the galley was equipped to prepare and serve full candlelight dinners. Full movie-projection facilities were laid on.

At least Harper made full use of it. Over one weekend he flew two senior creative people to Paris and back to give them a pep talk. Often the use was entirely personal, like when it was flown to Mexico to pick up antique furniture. And perhaps the one flight that was most symbolic of the impending disaster was when he used it to fly Valerie to France—on the day he was supposed to be in court on alleged tax offences.

Some of this could perhaps be tolerated if the company was performing, but the figures were ceasing to add up. At one time the organization employed 8,300 people worldwide with global billings of $711 million. But this growth by acquisition was hiding stagnation in trading. Neil Gilliatt, an account man and vice chairman in 1964 could remember "there were years in which the earnings on the Coca-Cola account were two or three times greater than the earnings of the total corporation."

Although the separation of the agencies allowed competing clients, there were some who still wouldn't play. The acquisition of Waseys with its Carnation business cost McCann's Nestlé, and McCann suffered again when Continental walked because of Jack Tinker taking on Braniff.

INCREASINGLY, HARPER WAS PUSHING the limits. Spielvogel had by now succeeded Stilson as one of the three trustees of the voting shares, along with Bob Healy and Harper. He remembers consulting a lawyer about an idea for the pension plan Harper had asked him to implement. "You do that Mr. Spielvogel," said the lawyer evenly, "and you see the stripes you're wearing on that suit? They'll be going the other way."

Harper wouldn't be told—he didn't believe he could fail. It all came to a head in 1967 when Irving Trust, worried by the balance sheet, called in a loan. Spielvogel, however, wasn't immediately worried. He had been advised by a financial mentor that the last thing banks wanted was to own any company, least of all a big advertising agency.

"So on that given day, on the fortieth floor of the TimeLife Building, Bob Healy and I were sitting there waiting for these four people from the Irving Trust who came in looking like four morticians and they said, 'We've very bad news for you. We're calling your loans', and I said 'Fine', and took out this big set of fake keys and put them on the table and we started to walk out. The lead banker said, 'Woah, where are you going?' and I said, 'You now own the largest advertising agency'. And he said, 'No, no, I'm sure we can work this out.'" They bought time from Irving Trust but with one condition—that Harper be removed from the chief executive position.

At promptly 10:00 AM on Thursday, November 9, 1967, a board meeting was called to order. Harper didn't seem to know what was about to hit him. He opened the meeting in the normal way but was quickly interrupted. The position of Irving Trust was outlined and Harper, puzzled but still apparently confident, put it to the vote.

All six men wordlessly voted against him. He paused for a moment and then, without saying a word, left the room.

Healy was installed as CEO, with Harper as chairman, but the board knew that their time with Irving Trust was limited. Arrangements were made with Chase Manhattan to refinance the agency but they in turn stipulated that Harper must go altogether. It was over.

Three clients, Coca-Cola, Heublien and Carnation, advanced $5 million in billings in a warming show of support and confidence. Within six months the business was in good shape.

Harper himself made two attempts to carry on in the business, the one at Harper, Rosenfeld & Sirowitz as a sort of Jack Tinker reincarnation, and the other as a marketing consultant. Neither worked out and he literally disappeared off the scene. Stories of tax fraud swirled around but nothing ever came to a head.

There is a strange Howard Hughes-like postscript to this story. In 1979, an *Advertising Age* reporter, John Revett, went down to Oklahoma City to see Harper's mother in an attempt to locate and possibly interview him. They were chatting away when a tall man walked into the room, asked who the interloper was and identified himself.

"I'm Marion Harper."

He didn't want to discuss the past.

10 Women of the Avenue

"Be a woman. It's a powerful business when done correctly."

BOBBIE BARRETT TO PEGGY OLSEN **MAD MEN**

Twenty-four-year-old Mary Moore, "all hair, and legs for miles," keen and fresh from a night course at the School of Visual Arts, sat in front of a senior art director who was looking for an assistant. She'd borrowed clothes for the interview from a colleague at the bank where she worked but had tried them on only that morning: "They were so tight. It was salacious. Every curve. And I had a nice coat so I thought I'm not going to take it off. I had a little rehearsal: 'Would you like to take your coat off?' 'No I'm a little chilly, I'll keep it on.' So that's what I did. And then he said, 'I wanna see what you look like. Stand up, do a twirl.' It was a strange feeling. I didn't know any better. I hadn't heard the drill—you don't do that. I knew this wasn't exactly right, but I couldn't imagine saying no. I figured maybe he was entitled to look at his employees."

It's a common story, right across the business—nothing physical but a casual sexism, low key harassment. Carl Ally openly encouraged intra-office flirting and relationships in the belief that it kept up interest levels in life at the agency—and thus attendance. Jerry Della Femina later shared that view, running his agency like a frat house with a lot of lusty males running around in lewd good humor.

"The men in those days took a lot of liberties with women: 'Look at the buns on that one,' 'Look at the chest on that one,' very blatant," says Mary

Leigh Weiss who worked at the Hooper Research organization. "You weren't offended, you were flattered. That's how it was in those days. Everyone wanted to be noticed by men, and they noticed you and you were flattered."

Not every woman would have agreed with that, but at the same time there's less rancor or bitterness about the gender attitudes than may be expected. According to Della Femina, the women were just as enthusiastic about the annual Sex Contest as the men. As Mary Moore says of what would now be seen as her utter humiliation that day, "I didn't go home in tears about it." It wasn't until 1963 that Betty Freidan's *The Feminine Mystique* was published and the awakening of consciousness amongst women started the long push for change.

When you talk about it now, most of the men will grin, albeit a little sheepishly, and the women just shrug, both sexes sometimes with a little gleam in the eye. Mary Moore remembers, "As I know, nobody nailed you in the ladies' room but there was a lot of talk about it and you constantly had to giggle." As one former secretary said, "It was just the way it was."

The overwhelming majority of the females available for flirtation were support staff, secretaries, and admin people. As with any minority group in advertising, no matter how enlightened the employment policy of any agency, it could move only at the pace of its clients, some of whom in the sixties were still specifying no Jews. And despite more than 50 percent of advertising always having been aimed at women, with a conservative, male-dominated client community it's difficult to find many reports of women account executives before 1960. Fashion and cosmetic accounts may have had the occasional female client and so occasionally an agency would employ a woman to work with her.

EVEN IN THE 1960s female account executives were few and far between, and it probably wasn't an appealing job for women anyway, the prevailing service culture generally involving hard drinking and racy entertainment. But this affected the creative people less as the clients didn't have to meet them or socialize with them.

There had always been female copywriters, even back in the nineteenth century; their three regular routes into the copy department were through a job writing for the vast number and variety of women's magazines, through an in-house writing job at a retail store, or starting as an agency secretary and transferring.

Even back in 1910 JWT had a women's unit, staffed by women copywriters headed by Helen Landsdowne. She had formidable talents, in writing, in business, and socially. In 1911 she wrote an ad for Woodbury's facial soap that both shocked and thrilled and is generally reckoned to represent the beginning of sex appeal in selling, with its visual of a man and a woman in close proximity, and the line "The skin you love to touch." She was a prominent suffragette and having married Stanley Resor, with whom she bought JWT from Commodore Thompson himself, became energetic in furthering the interests of women in business from a powerful position at the very top of the largest agency in the United States.

Bernice Fitzgibbon worked at Macy's from 1926 until 1940, when she moved to Gimbels where she ran their advertising department until 1954, with a significant number of female agency writers of the fifties and sixties passing through her department. Shirley Polykoff at FCB, one of a growing group of female copy chiefs and creative directors, gained national fame as the writer of "Does she or doesn't she?", the phenomenally successful Clairol hair colorant ad that raised eyebrows because of its sexual innuendo. Jane Trahey, a copywriter, started her own agency in 1960, a business and financial, if not high-profile, success. And for a while the DDB creative department under Phyllis Robinson had more women than men.

Women were particularly well represented in research departments but, apart from copywriting and the traditional areas of secretarial and clerical roles, there were very few other posts held by women. Even in art direction, a job for which gender should have been no more an issue than copywriting, women were almost nonexistent. As he recalls waiting for his interview at Benton & Bowles reception in 1961, Amil Gargano describes, "A young woman with long dark hair and brown eyes passed in front of me without glancing up from the paper she was reading. She was one of the most beautiful women I had ever seen." She was Elaine Parfundi and he's seen her more or less every day since as they married in December 1963. She was then the only female art director at Benton & Bowles and when she left six years later there was still only one other there.

Does
she...or
doesn't
She?

Hair color so natural only her hairdresser knows for sure!™

On a clear crisp day, in brightest sunlight, or in the soft glow of a candle, she always looks radiant, wonderfully natural. Her hair sparkles with life. The color young and fresh, as though she's found the secret of making time stand still. And in a way she has. It's Miss Clairol, the most beautiful, the most effective way to cover gray and to liven or brighten fading hair color.

Keeps hair in wonderful condition— soft, lively—because Miss Clairol carries the color deep into the hair shaft to shine outward, just the way natural hair color does. That's why hairdressers everywhere recommend Miss Clairol and more women use it than all other haircolorings. So quick and easy. Try it MISS CLAIROL yourself. Today. *HAIR COLOR BATH is a trademark of Clairol Inc. © Clairol Inc. 1962*

Even close up, Miss Clairol looks natural. The hair shiny, bouncy, the gray completely covered with the younger, brighter, lasting color no other kind of hair-coloring can promise —and live up to!

ABOVE *The advertisement for Clairol by Shirley Polyakoff at Foote, Cone & Belding, created in 1957.*

In the mid–1950s, Joy Golden was in the steno pool at BBDO with forty other girls, on $40 a week,with a supervisor walking up and down and all the typing you could handle. But in her lunchtime, just like Bill Bernbach years before at Schenley's, she decided to have a go at improving the ads she saw in *The Ladies' Home Journal*.

She wandered around the management floor with a sheaf of her ideas, looking for someone to show them to. Eventually she found Jean Rindlaub, a copy chief who liked what she saw and took Joy on as a copywriter. It was her first step on a lifetime career in the business, culminating with her own radio production company in the 1980s. Peggy Olsen's path in *Mad Men* had been trodden many times before by women like Joy.

HOWEVER GOOD THEY WERE at their jobs, women in any discipline at any level couldn't escape unequal treatment, some of it bizarre. According to advertising columnist Barbara Lippert, up until the sixties women working at BBDO weren't allowed in the executive dining room—a couple of senior female copywriters enjoyed the regal privilege of being served the meal at their desks from a silver cart by a maid in full uniform.

Attitudes to clothing and appearance too were still often deeply conservative. Joelle Anderson, in the research department at Grey, found it a pretty relaxed atmosphere but people were shocked, "even agog about it" when her group leader turned up in a pant suit one day. Even at Carl Ally, liberated and modish as it was, Ally saw fit to send an all staff memo after one of his female staff wore pants to the office, saying, "I look askance, at girls who wear pants." Three days later he cheerfully rescinded it when, as Pat Langer says, "He realized you could see more of a slim woman's shape in tight fitting pants than in a skirt."

The worst inequalities were in both prospects and salary. There was an automatic assumption, discussed but rarely fought against, that women would get less money than their male equivalents. Mary Moore had a boyfriend, an art director, working at the same agency as her: "We used to talk about how we wanted to leave and get better jobs. He said, 'You're terrific, you ought to be making $12,000, and I ought to be making $14,000.'"

As for promotion to senior executive level, again apart from copywriting or research, the glass ceiling was so obvious it might as well have been iron. By 1960, McCann-Erickson, led by a comparatively woman friendly Marion Harper, had only six female vice presidents out of a total of a hundred. No agency was led by a woman unless it was started by her. And JWT, once prominent in promoting women, didn't appoint their first female senior vice president until 1973.

None of this was the slightest deterrent to Mary Wells, a determined, stylish, brown-eyed, female writer who, as George Lois said, "You could tell would never end up with wrinkles in a writer's tower."

Her 1967 response to suggestions of discrimination was typically robust; despite the blatant evidence all around her, she pronounced, "The idea about American men trying to keep women down in business is a bunch of hogwash. I've never been discriminated against in my life, and I think the women who have experienced it would have anyway—no matter if they were men, or cows, or what have you. Only the 'nuts and the kooks' are screaming like babies."

While successful women are under no compulsion to campaign on behalf of their fellow women, it's also probably not necessary to dump on them quite so heavily. Amelia Bassin, formerly advertising director of Fabergé, hit back in the speech she made as the American Advertising Federation's newly elected Advertising Woman of the Year in 1970: "I can well believe Miss Mary never got discriminated against. There is no privileged class in the world to compare with that of the beautiful woman. . . . It's difficult to tell if success has spoiled Mary Wells; but boy, is she ever spoiling success."

But what success. No advertising woman, before or since, has ever gone so far and traveled so fast as Mary Wells Lawrence.

SHE CAME TO NEW YORK as eighteen-year-old Mary Berg from her native Youngstown, Ohio, in 1947 with hopes of being an actress. She didn't get anywhere and slipped into advertising through the traditional route for female writers—a job in the publicity department at a store, in her case Macy's. From there she was briefly at McCann-Erickson and then Lennen & Newell where she coincided briefly for the first time with Lois. By now she was Mary Wells—but more usually Bunny Wells—married to an art director at OB&M, Bert Wells.

With her knowledge of the fashion industry and her exquisite sense of style, an asset which was to be of immeasurable use to her later and shaped much of what she achieved, she was hired by Phyllis Robinson at DDB on fashion business. Diligence and determination got her to group head status and she also earned respect as a writer. It was she who was largely responsible for the evocative French tourism campaign for which she'd been on extensive visits to France, starting a love affair with Europe that's lasted throughout her life.

She was completely at home at the creative Mecca of DDB when, in 1963, a call came out of the blue from Jack Tinker to join her at his think tank. Wells arrived before the Alka Seltzer win, when the agency was performing well as an ideas generator but with an unspectacular reputation and image. Tinker and Harper felt that she was the person to liven it up.

Tinker had already hired an art director, Stewart Green, who Wells linked up with a writer she brought from DDB, Dick Rich, and it was these two she led in the Alka Seltzer project. With its immediate and enormous success, Harper and Tinker's appointment of Wells had quickly been vindicated.

There is no question that she was a terrific choice; unphased by traditional ways of doing business, she set about regenerating the agency, hiring a stream of A-list creative people and paying them well over the rate to get the place buzzing and talked about.

One of Wells' many insights was the recognition that there were more impactful ways of gaining publicity than schmoozing the trade press at 21. As *Mad Men*'s Don Draper said, "If you don't like the conversation, change it." She had a fantastic talent on behalf of her clients, her agency, and herself of getting people to talk about the things she wanted talked about.

It helped that she was petite, highly attractive, witty, and articulate. Both men and women when describing her will almost inevitably refer to her "great legs." Her style for that time was more European than American, she dressed with French chic and to English ears there is a slight Englishness to her accent—not the ersatz English of someone trying too hard but the refined, cultured note reminiscent of Grace Kelly, a woman with whom, coincidentally, she was to become great friends.

ABOVE *Mary Wells Lawrence in 1970, the founder of Wells Rich Greene, the largest agency run by a woman at the time.*

Ken Roman recalls a speech she gave at the Harvard Business School Club when she had become president of her own agency. "We'd never seen a president, a female president of an agency. So there's all these MBAs sitting there and she gets up, she's in a smartly tailored suit and she looked so sophisticated. And they're waiting to see what happens. And she had a scarf on, and she slowly took off the scarf, smiled, and said, 'And that's all I'm going to take off'. It was so perfect. She had show business."

She had massive energy. While cool and sophisticated, she was not above masculine rough-and-tumble and was surrounded by a praetorian guard of young, male creative people who were dazzled by her. It's unquestionable she hypnotized people, male and female. There are colleagues from the 1960s who are still enthralled by her, and have massive respect and admiration for her—although affection is a little less evident. There's even a little whiff of fear. Getting people to talk about her even now is a little like asking around for information on a mafia Don: John will speak if Jill goes first. "Tell me what Jack says and I'll tell you if I agree with him." "Don't ask me about that, ask Joan."

Rumors of both random kindness and random ruthlessness circulate equally. One story, unconfirmed, placed her in her office late one afternoon, where she had summoned a creative team, while her make-up artist prepared her for an evening function. With her back to the team, she fired them through the reflection in her mirror.

Time and again you're told she was a marketing genius, that she had the most extraordinary insights into the minds of the consumer, no matter who or for what product. When later she won American Motors, the male creative staff couldn't wait to get their hands oily, believing that a car, and a fairly downmarket car at that, was not something Mary would understand. But within days of getting the assignment, she'd given them a detailed rundown of every model and its potential role in possible buyers' lives. Apparently, she was spot on.

NEXT FOR WELLS at Jack Tinker was another of those lucky bounces that seem to preface so many great breakthroughs. In a trip to the west coast to court Continental airlines, their executive vice president, Harding Lawrence, confided to Wells that he was about to leave to head up a little-known Texas airline, Braniff, and he'd rather Tinker saved themselves for that account. This led to one of the most famous airline campaigns of all time—and certainly the making of Mary Wells, in both creative and business terms.

Braniff had plenty of lucrative routes, particularly to Central and South America, but almost no awareness. And Lawrence had big ideas, including immediate investment in a new fleet, and thus an urgent need to sell seats, which could only be brought about by instant fame.

This is where Wells' superlative sense of not just style but the application of style came in. An airline is an airline—they fly the same planes, seat you in the same seats, serve the same food. And, as she noticed, they did it in a utilitarian, almost military style. These were the early days of the jet age, before flying became packagable as romantic. Indeed, as DDB had noted with El Al, most airline advertising tended to be little more than timetable publication—there wasn't much else to say. Y&R hadn't even started their emotional Wings of Man campaign for Eastern Airlines.

In her 2002 autobiography *A Big Life (in Advertising)*, Wells described her epiphany one morning when standing in a check-in line at Chicago airport. "Airlines had developed out of the military . . . planes were metallic or white with a stripe painted down the middle to make them look as if they could get up and fly. The terminals were greige. They had off-white walls, cheap stone or linoleum floors, grey metal benches, there were tacky signs stuck into walls . . . Stewardesses, as they were called, were dressed to look like nurses. . . . There were no interesting ideas, no place for your eyes to rest, nothing smart anywhere."

Color. That was the answer. Vibrant, raging, scintillating, Braniff planes would be like brilliant flying jewels, like no planes you'd ever seen before, each painted in a different vivid color. The fabrics would dazzle and the stewardesses would dress in the most outrageous outfits. Alexander Girard was hired to design the interiors, Emilio Pucci to create the outfits for the stewardesses—or hostesses as Braniff now called them. A flight on Braniff was to be a party. Ideas on ticketing, seating, and entertainment came thick and fast. Turning a flight into a fashion parade, the stewardesses would change their outfits four times on the longer routes.

It was, as the launch print ad said, "The End of the Plain Plane." Created by writer Charlie Moss and art director Phil Parker, the line was printed under a picture of air hostesses and flight crew standing like a flock of brilliantly colored exotic birds on the wing of a vivid blue Braniff 720. The payoff to the copy was perfect, it could have been another headline: "We won't get you there any faster—but it'll seem that way."

The commercial was a kaleidoscopic view of the preparation for the print ad photo shoot, with the movements of the various people getting into position choreographed for maximum vivacity. Others followed, one announcing the stewardesses' changes of costume as "The Air Strip."

The launch was a wild success. Five Braniff planes—blue, green, yellow, red, and turquoise—flew low and slow past a grandstand at Dallas airport filled with three hundred press from around the world. Acclaim followed from the passengers. To Wells' delight there were reports of people playing the game, trying to book tickets on the basis of the color of plane they might fly on, going for the full set of seven. Acclaim also followed from the advertising business.

The campaign was well underway when Wells dropped a bombshell on Tinker and Harper; she resigned in order to set up on her own agency. She had been given her first real taste of authority and autonomy, and Tinker was never going to confine her for long after that—there's a huge and heady difference between being one of many creative group heads within a large creative department, as she had been, and being the charismatic leader of a "hot" agency, as she'd now experienced.

How it came about is confused by several differing reports. In her autobiography Wells says she was furious because Harper reneged on a deal to make her president—a deal which curiously she hadn't previously noted in the book, but if had been made it was presumably offered as a lure to get her to join in the first place. Tinker, on the other hand, says she came to him suggesting they try to buy the agency out of Interpublic. He put a deal to Harper which was refused and, sensing she wouldn't stay much longer anyway, he agreed that she should set up her own company. Yet another version has Harper offering her the presidency but he was blocked by Hertzog and Myron McDonald, who said they would never work for her, and so she felt she had to leave. What is fact, however, is that through Carl Spielvogel, Harper offered her a contract worth $1 million over ten years, a quite phenomenal deal for 1966.

ABOVE *'The End of the Plain Plane'; in 1965 the Braniff image was completely reinvented by Mary Wells, Alexander Girard and Emilio Pucci.*

ABOVE AND OPPOSITE *Further examples from the Braniff campaign, including the "The Air Strip." Originally there were eight different colors for the aircraft but lavender when combined with white and black is bad luck in Mexico and South America, so the color scheme was dropped to seven.*

With some courage she refused the offer. With Dick Rich, Stew Greene, and, critically, the Branifff account, and actively encouraged by Harding Lawrence, who she would marry the next year, she set up Wells Rich Greene (WRG) in the Gotham Hotel in April 1966.

OF THE SUBSEQUENT SUCCESS, just a few figures need to be grasped. She started with the $6 million billing from Braniff, a loan from Chemical Bank and a handful of employees in four rooms at the Gotham, including her mother answering the phone. By the end of the first year her agency, now at 575 Madison Avenue, billed $35 million, and had a hundred employees. Within five years, WRG was billing $100 million with five offices, two of them overseas. Allowing for inflation, no stand alone start-up agency has ever exceeded that rate of growth. By 1969 Wells was paying herself $250,000 per year, a salary higher than anyone else in US advertising, man or woman. And when she took the company public in 1968, she became the first ever female CEO of a quoted company of any sort in US history.

And to remind ourselves just how far we've come in this story, the agency principles were a woman and two Jews—and all three creative people.

Divorced from Bert Wells as she started at Tinker, she married Harding Lawrence in Paris in 1967, a close marriage that lasted until his death in 2002. Typical of Wells was the exclusivity and originality of her wedding outfits. In the middle of this phenomenally demanding period she'd had time to spot Halston, a hat designer for Bergdorf Goodman, and asked him to design a green velvet wedding dress—green was a popular color with her. It was the first dress he ever sold. For the night before the wedding she wore a black ruffled and flounced organza creation made for her by Hubert de Givenchy. Style, always style.

Contributing to the agency's growth was the win of American Motors, some P&G business, and TWA, which she won after agreeing with her husband to drop Braniff. That account went to George Lois's new agency, Lois Holland Calloway, where he created the campaign "If you've got it, flaunt it," featuring amongst other commercials Andy Warhol explaining the finer points of his art to an impassive Sony Liston seated next to him on a Braniff flight.

Wells' first successful account was the return of an old friend, Alka Seltzer, which also boosted the billings. They had moved to DDB shortly after Wells, Rich, and Greene's breakaway from Tinker, triggering its sad implosion. DDB had given Alka Seltzer more wonderfully entertaining and memorable advertising but in the view of Miles Laboratories it was ineffective and too costly; DDB was insisting on sixty-second spots and the client wanted thirty seconds to double their exposure. They called Mary, and she gave them the thirty-second media schedule they wanted. She also gave them yet another string of memorable commercials: "Try it, you'll like it" and "I can't believe I ate the whole thing," both of which slogans passed into the national vernacular.

One of the earliest WRG gains was in the increasingly controversial category of tobacco. The advertising business had the same problem as government with what was now confirmed as a killer product; there was just too much money in it to walk away. And money brought exposure and thus possible fame for the agency's work. The Marlboro Cowboy, first run in 1955, had helped put Chicago's Leo Burnett on the national map. While some, like DDB and Carl Ally, refused to work on the deadly weed, Wells took the view that if it was permissible to sell it, it should be permissible to advertise it. Anything else was hypocrisy, "un-American" as she put it.

Philip Morris offered them Benson and Hedges 100s, a cigarette that was longer than king-size. They were expecting something cool and image-based, probably visual metaphors to do with longer slimmer objects—aircraft, skyscrapers, or, as they put it, long legs accentuated by mini skirts.

Once in front of their layout pads Rich and Greene agreed the brief was drivel and came up with an idea that couldn't have been sweeter or further away from Philip Morris' expectations: the disadvantages of the Benson and Hedges 100s. Like the Alka Seltzer "Stomachs" it was a series of close-ups, this time of people failing to come to grips with the extra length of the cigarette while smoking it. One man gets his jammed in an elevator door; another sets fire to the beard of the man he's talking to; one tries to light his two thirds of the way up; and in yet another we see a man's face obscured by the newspaper he's reading—a hole is slowly burnt in the page as his cigarette smolders its way through. By making them uncool, WRG made them—and themselves, as the brightest new agency on Madison Avenue—uber cool.

In a 2002 interview with USA today she said of her decision to handle tobacco accounts, "I wouldn't do it now. Based on the knowledge we have today, we'd make a different decision." She adds, "I don't feel I owe anyone an apology." Harding Lawrence, a heavy smoker, had died of emphysema and lung cancer a few months before.

NOT EVERYONE FOUND the agency and the act so captivating. There were of course the envious, the reactionary, and the mysoginistic. But there were also more serious critics who simply disliked Wells' perspective of the job of an advertising agency.

Says Amil Gargano, "The mention of her name would send Carl Ally into an unbridled rage. He thought she was a complete charlatan. He resented the fact that her best work was for a cigarette. Hated what she did for Braniff, the epitome of everything he loathed about her approach. Described her agency as 'The School of Fashion and Theatrics.'"

Well, yes, it was. She'd come to New York as an actress and theater was never far from her ideas. But she understood that there was no rule stating that the public shall respond only to the purity of a double page spread or the simplicity of a well-argued TV spot. They respond to theatrics too, and Wells' idea was to create spectacles and let them be the advertisement.

No one in her professional life knew her better than Charlie Moss. They first met at DDB, and he then worked with her from the Jack Tinker days until the absorption of WRG into another Harper-style consortium in 1998. His first impression of Mary, as it is for so many, had been of her style.

"DDB was linoleum floors, offices painted a drab white, steel desks in every office, and two directors chairs with the canvas backs, and a chair for the person who had the office. A typewriter if you were a writer, an art board if you were an art director, and one big, BIG cork board on your wall. . . . Now when I first met Mary, I was shocked because her inner sanctum was very different from the rest of the agency. It was the only office that was decorated. It had an orange floor, and a French provincial credenza [desk], it was actually civilized-looking. It was the only office like that in the entire agency as far as I knew apart from maybe Bernbach's upstairs."

Later, when interviewing for an art director at Tinker, she and Dick Rich had been impressed by a trade campaign for Rheingold beer in the book of DDB art director Phil Parker, who had been working with Moss. Moss takes up the story:

"The idea entailed telling people that Rheingold sponsored the Mets. The Mets were, at that time, a joke, they hadn't won a game in months, they were pathetic. And we came up with this idea that if the Mets won the pennant, we would buy everybody in NYC a beer. Then we changed it to buying everyone a beer if they won six games straight because the pennant would be out of the question. A beer party at Shea Stadium, everybody was invited, and Rheingold would sponsor it. But the Mets would not allow it to run. They felt it was making fun of them. It was withdrawn. The client loved it, everybody loved it. Anyways, it was what got me my job at Tinker. What it had in it inherently was a promotional aspect and that's what Mary was about. Take the French Tourist Bureau at DDB. She created [a new] French tourist industry by insisting that they turn chateaus into hotels, and really market what they had so that Americans would appreciate it. Her advertising was secondary to the product that she helped to create."

Most agencies when given the Braniff brief would have tried to find a persuasive argument to convince the traveler that the current Braniff was a better airline. Wells took it further; she took the airline apart, recreated it with fireworks, noise, and fun, and advertised that.

Advertising, and thus the advertising agency, is no longer about merely ads. Agencies have to be prepared to be about ideas that are above and beyond simple advertising. And as Mary Moore said of Mary Wells, with whom she worked in the seventies, "Her ideas were simply vast."

In that respect, she was an indicator of things to come. As with the revolutionaries at the start of the decade who had done so much to kickstart the upheaval and move on from the past, it was Mary Wells who was now bringing in the fresh thinking.

She was the embodiment of the advertising creative person to come. The pointer to the future.

"We're creative. The least important,
most important thing."

DON DRAPER TO PEGGY OLSEN **MAD MEN**

It had to be that particular period in which all this happened,
mainly for economic and social reasons but also for one rather more joyful
factor: in that decade there was an attitude of "anything goes," and so
anything went, including a gigantic beneficent canvas across which to
experiment, explore, and sometimes gloriously fail. Optimism, energy,
creativity, and hope were so abundant that circumstances that in any other
era would have triggered gloom and despair, inspired instead capricious
defiant laughter and scintillating new ideas. But these circumstances
changed as a darkness began to fall on the end of the sixties.

On the morning of March 6, 1970, a series of explosions ripped through
the bare branches of the trees on West Eleventh Street, just off Fifth
Avenue. As the smoke and dust cleared, it revealed No 18, one of the elegant
town houses lining the street, as a burning ruin. Shortly after, two stunned
young women, one naked, the other barely clothed and both covered in
dust and debris, asked at a neighbor's house for help. They were given
coffee and clothes and then, while firemen and police were going through
the rubble next door, they disappeared. The two women were Kathy Boudin
and Cathy Wilkerson—and neither was seen again for ten years.

Over the next few days the scattered body parts of two men and a woman
were gathered from the wreckage and the story begun to emerge. The five

were members of the Weathermen, a faction of the Students for a Democratic Society, and the basement kitchen had been turned into a bomb factory. They'd stockpiled a massive supply of dynamite, preparing bombs that were to be detonated in a Vietnam war protest at an officer cadet dance at Fort Dix that evening, but someone made a mistake.

The event is tragically symbolic of the end of the bubbly, sun-dappled decade. The house belonged to Wilkerson's father, and was empty because he had been away on business. He was the European Head of Y&R.

While their fathers were still gambolling happily in advertising's rich pasture, the coming generation was increasingly disaffected, "down in the basement, mixing up the medicine . . . you don't need a Weatherman to see the way the wind blows," as Dylan had prophetically written five years earlier. The bombing was one of an accelerating list of menacing events, big and small, ushering in the seventies.

The Chicago 1968 Democratic Convention, which erupted in vicious riots and bloodshed with a mayor and a police force out of control, had brought mainstream political life to a corrupt and homicidal low, a sickening contrast to the high on which the decade had started with the election of a new young president.

Any validity the hippy and drug-oriented alternative society could have claimed was disintegrating fast. The deranged August 1969 Manson family killings and the escalating violence at the Altamont concert in December 1969, which ended with the murder of a fan by the Hell's Angels "security force" at the feet of the Rolling Stones, had eclipsed the dreamy peace and love of Woodstock only four months earlier.

The simultaneous realization of the futility, the disgrace, and the horror of the Vietnam war, with the apocalyptic escalation of US casualties in 1967 and 1968 was creating endless antagonisms and self-doubt throughout American society. And right on Madison Avenue's own doorstep, New York City itself was becoming drug-ridden, dangerous, filthy, and desperately broke.

US business entered a mini depression, and advertisers began to cut back. So the renegades were beginning to have a tougher time in a harder, more cynical environment. And if following a revolution there is no counterrevolution, the new state becomes the status quo. It wasn't quite like that with the Creative Revolution, for although the new ways of thinking and working took hold across the business, the old ways weren't by any means vanquished.

So here, at 1970, with the initial skirmishes over and no clear winner, it would seem to be a good time to take stock of the situation.

FROM AMONGST THE CAST of Madison Avenue, the previous twenty years had thrown up plenty of huge characters; acclaimed for bringing a very high standard to existing roles. But those roles were redefined by Bill Bernbach and the framework within which they were performed was redesigned by Marion Harper. It's therefore no surprise that in their "1999 Review of the Advertising Century," *Advertising Age* cited these two as the most influential figures of the entire twentieth century. They put Bernbach first. But—and as a lifelong copywriter who has just about worshipped Bernbach since the day I first became aware of what he stood for, this is not easy to say—I'm not so sure.

Undoubtedly, the overall standard of creative work around the world improved. Yes, there was, and still is, absolute dross and plenty of it—not until the twenty-first century did P&G take the least notice of anything Bernbach had said—but overall there was a greater attempt to meet the consumers halfway. And it was a lasting improvement. Tiresome arguments with clients about whether or not humor sells or the wisdom of portraying women as anything other than attachments to household appliances became easier to win when there was the example of DDB and other agencies' commercial success with a wittier, cleverer strain of work.

But would this have happened anyway? The social pressures were so powerful at the beginning of the sixties and the simple youthful majority were so voluble and irresistible that surely, sooner or later, the forces would have been marshalled and brought about a revolution in the way agencies communicated with the public?

And there were negative outcomes to the revolution. Amongst those new agencies there were a lot of failures in both structure and output. Creative idealism was proving to be a far from adequate sole qualification for agency momentum and when it came to the work, too many of the young creative pretenders understood all of the fun and none of the discipline of Bernbach's style. They knew how to grab attention and entertain, but they forgot that the whole point was to persuade.

This was not Bernbach's fault, far from it. The silliness and the self-indulgence hiding behind "creativity" in some of the newer work was the despair of DDB and other new agencies like Carl Ally. According to Bob Levinson, Bernbach said, "Our job is to sell our clients" merchandise . . . not ourselves. Our job is to kill the cleverness that makes us shine instead of the product." Old school detractors of the new creativity could point to this lack of discipline as evidence of flaws at the heart of the new creative ideal. And frequently, it *was* a flaw.

Further, the revolution itself was far from total. The so called "creative agencies" spent approximately only 8 percent of the total US billing through the decade, almost insignificant in commercial terms. Remove DDB from that equation and the figure becomes negligible. Yes the takeover was total in advertising award shows and internal regard—advertising has always been narcissistic—but the big, old agencies powered on much as they always had.

As to the detail of Bernbach's innovations, there had been precedents. As long ago as 1902 a New York agency set up by Ralph Holden, an account man, and Earnest Elmo Calkins, a copywriter, was promoting the role of the art directors and teaming them with the copywriters in meetings described by the agency as "The Composite Man." It was to achieve what Calkins described as "that combination of text with design that produces a complete advertisement."

Calkins gained a reputation as a great shepherd of creative people, unusually for a copywriter, sponsoring photography and new and original illustrators. He was the first true creative director and the agency's softer, more considered approach gathered plenty of admirers from within advertising circles, *Printer's Ink* magazine praising them in 1904 for producing "the finest art work of any agency in New York at the time."

Although almost certainly accidental, it is a template for the DDB of nearly fifty years later and it shows that the marriage of art director with writer was not entirely new. It seems that Bernbach also had a philosophical model in Raymond Rubicam, as Y&R in the years up to World War II produced a stream of intelligent, imaginative, and honest work. Bernbach wouldn't deny this—he once told Rubicam, "I don't think

I could have quite made it without your influences," Rubicam having personally articulated much of Bernbach's credo. He elevated the creative people within his agency, respected the art director and championed original creative work. Like DDB later, a place in Rubicam's creative department was so prized that one writer earning of $9,000 per year at Y&R turned down an offer of $25,000 from a rival agency while another said, "We were Y&R and that meant the best there was. It was more of a religion than it was an advertising agency."

Across the century there were plenty of industry leaders making sensitive observations about a need to raise the respect shown to the consumer in the quality of advertising. Emerson Foote, Albert Lasker, Theodore MacManus, Leo Burnett all spoke Bernbach's language. Even at the end of the nineteenth century, Minnie Maude Hanff, the writer in an all-female team creating ads for Force Breakfast, had shown a realistic appraisal of the public's relationship to selling by saying, "Goodness gracious! A breakfast food isn't all life is it? People are not going to take it nearly as seriously as the advertiser wants them to."

So Bernbach's philosophy wasn't entirely new. The difference is that he was the first one to take these ideals and do much of anything about them—and make an impact that lasts to this day. That gives him his monumental place in history.

HARPER'S INFLUENCE, unlike Bernbach's, is indiscernible to the lay person. But whether we like it or not—and I don't for reasons I'll try to explain—his shadow is sharper and further reaching than Bernbach's. You need look at only one fact to get the point: what is DDB today but a part—a very large part but a part nevertheless—of exactly the sort of conglomerate that Harper dreamed up? Indeed, where are *any* of the Creative Revolution agencies now? Those enterprises started with such passion and vision, PKL, A&G, Scali McCabe Sloves, Ammirati and Puris, WRG . . . Gone, all gone, sold to the conglomerates that were the gleam in Harper's eye.

No one had had Harper's idea before and nothing else has changed the organization and operation of advertising as much. From what was largely a cottage industry of small privately owned shops competing in local markets with a personalized service delivering advertising only, the business has been through the equivalent of its own industrial revolution.

Employing any one of the squadrons of specialist companies owned by the massive global conglomerates, a client can now buy any and every conceivable service remotely connected with marketing, from research to strategic planning, from social network promotions to brand design.

Today, more than two-thirds of total US marketing services revenue goes to one or other of the advertising conglomerates, vast companies like Harper's own Interpublic, WPP, Publicis, Omnicom, Aegis, Havas, and MDC Partners. Of course, Harper is not responsible for the precise ways in which his vision has evolved or the business is now conducted but his template is the template from which the bulk of the industry now operates.

It is rare now to find any major agency in any country that is autonomous; major decisions are usually made thousands of miles away. And as all the major groups are publicly quoted, their emphasis is very much on the bottom line. With the quarterly reporting periods that are the death of coherent long-term planning, and a top level of management who were once absorbed in clients and their problems but are now hypnotized by Wall Street and the stockholders, you have a business with its priorities in the wrong place.

Almost without exception the leaders of the Creative Revolution agencies at some time or another expressed regret at going public. Both Grey and Mary Wells bought their companies back quite soon after selling stock, Wells saying the flotation was a waste of time. Papert and Lois certainly wished they could have recovered theirs but it was too late. We can be cynical and say these principals were happy to pocket the conglomerates' or investors' money but that's apart from the point to be made.

The quality of their work stuttered and fell away as they stopped being what they were good at and tried to be something else. Even the saintly DDB went through extraordinary contortions once they saw themselves as a "grown-up" business in 1970, acquiring Snark Products Inc., a small New Jersey-based manfacturer of plastic-hulled sailboats, believing the Snark would become the "VW of the sea." It didn't. They also tried to buy Frose-Mar Corp, an ice cream company. James Madden, senior VP, of DDB's Diversified Services unit, once said that in a six-month period he had looked at 300 potential acquisitions.

Of course, it is a business—does any of this idealistic handwringing matter? Yes, it does; creative endeavor will never fully flourish when the only imperative is profit. It loses sight of the fact that, as this tale shows, advertising is entirely about people. There is nothing else, no plant and equipment, no raw materials—it's just people and their ideas. And people, especially creative people, are not always fuelled by money alone.

Further, the contemporary advertising business has painted itself into a corner where there is no financial or emotional tolerance for failure. A creative endeavor without room for mistakes is a contradiction in terms; it's almost inconceivable that you can be as original as Bill Bernbach demanded without occasionally failing.

There has been another unforeseen consequence of the mass flotation. The propensity for the conglomerates to buy has created a supply, from the seventies onward, of agencies set up with the sole purpose of growing as quickly as possible, by any means, and then selling for a quick kill. Contrast that as a mission and a motivation with the zeal for advertisements of a Bernbach, a Lois, or a Carl Ally.

Can the two ideas live side by side? Omnicom worldwide can probably lay claim to having best combined Bernbach's creative vision with Harper's business idea. When they were building their network from the seventies onward they bought carefully, picking up local agencies only with proven creative credentials and allowing them reasonable autonomy. It is not insignificant that it is Omnicom who today own BBDO—and DDB. As a consequence, like the DDB of the *Mad Men* era, the Omnicom agencies tend to produce the better work and they do good business.

AND WHAT OF THE REAL Mad Men and Women? How do they view that curious era, an era that now seems like a sabbatical between conformity and uniformity?

In the fifteen months I took to write this book I interviewed or consulted well over fifty veterans of Madison Avenue, men and women. Admittedly I did concentrate mainly on those involved in the newer exciting agencies, for that is where the story lies. With only one mild exception not one expressed any regret about the time they'd spent and the work they'd done—far from it. Funny, witty, entertaining, sharp, and articulate, they looked back with enormous fondness and even respect for what the era had brought them.

What they brought to the era was a new deal on advertising. With their inbuilt aversion to phoniness and hype, they found it deeply difficult to concoct advertising on the basis of its accepted but shallow appeal—aspiration. You didn't drive a VW or a Volvo, smoke B&H 100s, holiday in Jamaica, eat at Horn and Hardart, or rent a car from Avis because you aspired to it or because it got you the girl or made you the envy of your neighbors. You did it because it was the clever thing to do. Advertising still told you that to be seen doing these things flattered you, yes, but where it used to flatter your status or your apparent wealth, now it flattered your intelligence. And it did this in an intelligent way, without treating you like an automaton or a fool. DDB and PKL and Carl Ally and the many that followed removed banality and aspiration from advertising.

That fifty years later those veterans still argue passionately over who should be credited for which ads can be read either as a sign of senior grumpiness or lasting pride and passion. I shall take it as the latter—and at least it was usually done with style and humor, as with one copywriter warning me off what he saw as his former art director's attempts to steal all his thunder: "paraphrasing Mary McCarthy on Lillian Hellman; 'everything he writes is a lie, even 'and' and 'but'.'"

Their reaction to their portrayal on *Mad Men* is a different matter. Uniformly, they loathed the first few episodes so much so that many have not returned to the series. They were offended more at the portrayal of the dishonesty and double dealing than they were at the drinking and fornicating. In the summer of 2010, George Lois wrote a furious piece for *Playboy* magazine that was openly hostile to everyone involved in the production. But others, like Mike Tesch, a one-time art director at Carl Ally, changed their minds as the series developed: "I hated it . . . then I loved it."

One thing of which they are all equally contemptuous is the output of Sterling Cooper. But then they have every right. None of them would ever have wanted to work for Draper and none of his department would have got a job at any of their agencies. Particularly Draper himself.

Too phony.

Bibliography

Abbott David and Marcantonio, Alfredo. *Remember Those Great Volkswagen Ads?*, Harriman House Ltd, 2008.

"Advertising: Adman's Adman," *Time Inc.*, March 31, 1958.

"Advertising: The Mammoth Mirror," *Time Inc.*, October 12, 1962.

"Advertising: The Big Ten Still Shine," *Time Inc.*, April 12, 1968.

"The Advertising Century," *Advertising Age*, Special Issue, 1999.

Art Direction Magazine, throughout the 1960s.

Art Directors Club of New York. *The Annuals of Advertising and Editorial Art and Design*, 1959–1970.

Challis, Clive. *Helmut Krone: The Book*, Cambridge Enchorial Press, 2005.

Cummings, Bart. *The Benevolent Dictators*, NTC Business Books, 1984.

DDB News, November 1972.

DDB News, 25th Anniversary Edition, June 1974, interview with Phyllis Robinson and Bob Gage.

Delaney, Sam. *Get Smashed: The Story of the Men Who Made the Adverts That Changed Our Lives*, Hodder & Stoughton, 2007.

Della Femina, Jerry. *From Those Wonderful Folks Who Gave You Pearl Harbor*, Simon and Schuster, 1970.

"Designs for Living," *Playboy Magazine*, July 1961.

Dillon, Jack. *The Advertising Man*, Fawcett Crest Publications, 1973.

Dobrow, Larry. *When Advertising Tried Harder*, Friendly Press Inc., 1984.

Dusenberry, Phil. *And Then We Set His Hair On Fire*, Portfolio Hardcover, 2005.

Fletcher, Winston. *Powers of Persuasion*, Oxford University Press, 2008.

Fox, Stephen. *The Mirror Makers*, University of Illinois Press, 1997.

Frank, Thomas. *The Conquest of Cool*, The University of Chicago Press, 1997.

Fryburger, Vernon. *The New World of Advertising*, Crain Books, 1975.

Gargano, Amil. *Ally & Gargano*, Graphics US Inc, 2010.

Gilbert, Richard. *Marching Up Madison Avenue*, Behler Publications, 2008.

Ginsberg, Allen. "Howl," in *Howl and Other Poems*, City Lights Publisher, reissue edition, 2010.

Glatzer, Robert. *The New Advertising*, Citadel Press, 1970.

Goodis, Jerry. *Have I Ever Lied To You Before?*, McClelland and Stewart, 1972.

Herzburn, David. *Playing in Traffic on Madison Avenue*, Business One Irwin, 1990.

Higgins, Denis. *The Art of Writing Advertising*, McGraw-Hill Contemporary, 1965.

Johnston, Russ. *Marion Harper— An Unauthorized Biography*, Crain Books, 1982.

Klaw, Spencer. 'What is Marion Harper Saying?', *For Some the Dream Came True*, edited by Duncan Norton Taylor, Lyle Stuart, 1986.

Kelly, James. *The Insider*, Henry Holt and Co, New York, 1958.

Lawrence, Mary Wells. *A Big Life in Advertising*, Touchstone, 2003.

Levenson, Bob. *Bill Bernbach's Book*, Villard, 1987.

Lois, George. *George, Be Careful*, Saturday Review Press, 1972.

"Madison Avenue: Advertising's Creative Explosion," *Newsweek*, August 18, 1961.

Mayer, Martin. *Madison Avenue U.S.A.*, Penguin Books, 1958.

McLean, Jesse. *Kings of Madison Avenue*, ECW Press, 2009.

Messner, Tom. "The Old Testament," *Ad Week*, January 16, 2006.

Messner, Tom. "The New Testament," *Ad Week*, December 12, 2005.

Meyer, Jackie Merri. *Mad Ave: Award-winning Advertising of the Twentieth Century*, Universe Publishing, 2000.

Millman, Nancy. *Emperors of Adland*, Warner Books, 1988.

Nulty, Peter. 'An aging boy wonder shakes up the ad business', *Fortune* April 13, 1987

Ogilvy, David. *Confessions of an Advertising Man*, Southbank Publishing, 2004.

Ogilvy, David. *Ogilvy On Advertising*, Prion, 2007.

O'Reilly Terry and Tennant, Mike. *The Age of Persuasion: How Marketing Ate Our Culture*, Knopf Canada, 2009.

Packard, Vance. *The Hidden Persuaders*, Pelican Books, 1962.

Reeves, Rosser. *Reality in Advertising*, Knopf, 1961.

Rielly, Edward J. *The 1960s: American Popular Culture in History*, Greenwood Press, 2003.

Ries, Al and Trout, Jack. *Positioning: The Battle For Your Mind*, McGraw-Hill, 2001.

Roman, Kenneth. *The King of Madison Avenue: David Ogilvy and the Making of Modern Advertising*, Palgrave Macmillan, 2009.

Rothenberg, Randall. *Where The Suckers Moon: The Life and Death of an Advertising Campaign*, Vintage Books, 1994.

Sullivan, Luke. *A Guide to Creating Great Ads*, John Wiley & Sons, 2003.

Tungate, Mark. *Adland*, Kogan Page, 2007.

Twitchell, James B. *Twenty Ads That Shook The World*, Three Rivers Press, 2000.

"US Business: The Men On The Cover: Advertising," *Time Inc.*, October 12, 1962.

Wakeman, Frederic. *The Hucksters*, Rinehart & Company Inc., 1946.

Willens, Doris. *Nobody's Perfect: Bill Bernbach and the Golden Age of Advertising*, Create Space, 2009.

Online and other media

Advertising Collection and Museums, part of the Advertising Educational Doundation.

"Art & Copy" [documentary], directed by Doug Pray, The One Club, 2010.

Art Directors Club Hall of Fame citations.

Curtis, Adam. "Experiments in the Laboratory of Consumerism," *BBC.co.uk*, 2010.

Ephron, Erwin. *Comfort the Afflicted, Afflict the Comfortable*, Ephron on Media, November 5, 2008.

Fitzgerald, Jeff, 'The Genius Guide to Jazz: Rondo', AllAboutJazz.com, May 2001.

"From the Great Depression Through the Great Recession: A Brief History of Marketing," *Adage.com*, March 29, 2010.

Lois, George. "On leaving DDB and the Creative Revolution," *Thebuzzbubble.com*, February 4, 2010.

"History: 1960s," *Adage.com*, September 15, 2003.

Imseng, Dominik. "George Lois on the Creative Revolution," 2009, www.youtube.com/.

Klaassen, Abbey. "Covering the Mad Men: Advertsing Age at 40," *Adage.com*, March 29, 2010.

Lippert, Barbara. "Mad Men with Tom Messner," *Adweek.com*, August 5, 2008.

Nishio, Tadashi, Articles about Great Creators, http://d.hatena.ne.jp/chuukyuu/.

Q&A with Matthew Weiner, *AMCTV.com*.

"Out of the Ordinary," [documentary] directed by Peter Simonson, www.outofthequestion.org.

Ross, Helen Klein. "Ad broad who invented the lemon," *Ad broad on Blogspot.com*, July 2, 2009.

The 30 Second Candidate: Rosser Reeves Collection, www.pbs.com.

"Selling the Sixties," [documentary] directed by Tim Kirby, BBC, 2008.

Solmon, Gregory. "Q&A: Jerry Della Femina," *AdWeek.com*, June 16, 2008.

The John W. Hartman Center for Sales, Marketing and Advertising History at Duke University Libraries, "Not Just Mad Men: Real advertising careers in the 1960's," [online video] November 10, 2008.

"This American Life," [radio program] *Episode 383: Sarah Koenig*, www.thisamericanlife.org.

Acknowledgments

This book is built on a giant heap of thoughts and ideas and help from a wide range of people, all of whom have my gratitude and respect. I've tried to remember you all. Please forgive me if I left you out and put it down to disorganization rather than indifference. My thanks and appreciation go to you and;

IN NEW YORK Fred Danzig and Marsha Cohen for research, reading the text, and many good insights and advice; Fiona Carter and Steve Zaroff for hospitality and encouragement; Tom Nelson, Steve Gardner, and Mel Moody at Gardner Nelson & Partners for use of their office, for help, and free coffee; Mary Warlick at The One Club for initial help and ideas; Jamie Pastor Bolnick for loan of her original City Lights imprint of Allen Ginsberg's "Howl"; Marsha Appel and her Research Staff at the 4As for facts and figures; and the Art Directors Club for review of their annuals.

IN LONDON James Garrett and William Eccleshare for reading every word and telling me, gently and constructively, what they thought of it; Amy Cracknell for transcripts; and all at Elwin Street Productions for patience and latitude.

IN WALES Richard and Maggie Sage (Manser), and Laura Hill, for laughs and a refuge to write at Werngochlyn Farm through the hard winter of 2010/2011 – and to Maggie for reading the manuscript.

Then there are the veterans of the creative revolution themselves, older, wiser, and probably funnier even than they were then; ever helpful, ever courteous, and ever fascinating. If the writing was at times irksome, the interviewing was always riveting and often hilarious. I thank you all for your time, understanding, and enthusiasm to fill in the blanks.

FROM EUROPE David Abbott, David Ashwell, Martin Boase, Jeremy Bullmore, Tim Delaney, Carl Hahn, Sir John Hegarty, Alfredo Marcantonio, Peter Mayle, Sir Alan Parker, John Salmon, Sir Nigel Seeley, Dave Trott

FROM THE US Doug Alligood, Joelle Anderson, Thelma Anderson, John Bernbach, Terry Bonaccolta, Bruce Crawford, Larry Dobrow, Jim Durfee, Erwin Ephron, Jerry Della Femina, Carl Fischer, Elaine Gargano, Phil Geier, Richard Gilbert, Bob Giraldi, Joy Golden, George Gomes, Ron Holland, Julian Koenig, Andy Langer, Pat Langer, Ed McCabe, Tom Messner, Mary Moore, Charlie Moss, Fred Papert, Terry Player, Martin Puris, Jim Raniere, Harriet Reisen, Al Ries, Ken Roman, Allen Rosenshine, Helen Klein Ross, Ted Shaine, Carl Spielvogel, Helayne Spivak, Mike Tesch, Judy Wald, Mary Leah Weiss

AND IN PARTICULAR, Amil Gargano, Bob Kuperman and George Lois, who never flagged when time and again I went back with "one last question."

Index

Note: Page numbers in *italics* refer to illustrations.

Carl Ally

Jerry Della Femina and Partners

Ron Rosenfeld,
creative director,
J. Walter Thompson